How to Get in Football Shape

CONDITIONING

Front cover image provided by Corbis Images.
Back cover photography and all black and white photography,
excluding DVD grabs, provided by Keith Hadley.

"The Benefits of Conditioning," compiled by and reprinted with permission from:
Michael Olpin
Assistant Professor Health and Human Performance
Weber State University
Ogden, Utah 84408
Web page: faculty.weber.edu/molpin/
Web address: molpin@weber.edu

How to Get in Football Shape: Strength Training by Bert Hill, and *How to Grow a Winning Quarterback* by Jerry Rhome, published by Cool Springs Press, Nashville, Tennessee, 2003.

Astroturf® is a registered trademark of Southwest Recreational Industries.

Published by Cool Springs Press, a Division of Thomas Nelson, Inc.,
P.O. Box 141000, Nashville, Tennessee, 37214

Library of Congress Cataloging-in-Publication Data is available.
ISBN 1-591860-04-0

First printing 2003
Printed in the United States of America
10 9 8 7 6 5 4 3 2 1

Editor: Ramona D. Wilkes
Copyeditor: Jason Zasky
Proofing: Sally Graham
Production/Design: Joey McNair of Defy Creative

Visit the Thomas Nelson website at www.ThomasNelson.com

The National Football League Coaches Association Presents

How to Get in Football Shape

CONDITIONING

FOR BOYS 14 AND OLDER

BERT HILL
STEVE WATTERSON

COOL
SPRINGS
PRESS

Nashville, Tennessee
A Division of Thomas Nelson, Inc.
www.ThomasNelson.com

Contents

Foreword

O n behalf of the National Football League Coaches Association (NFLCA), I am proud to present this book to young athletes across America. It's one of many projects undertaken by the NFLCA that provide tomorrow's high school and college players with proven fundamentals that work on the field and off, in the classroom and at home.

The NFLCA was founded in 1996 primarily to assist retired NFL coaches with issues such as salary, insurance, pensions and other benefits. But the educational and instructional aspect of our work has blossomed in recent years. To date, we have published three instructional books for youths. Our coaches participate in innumerable clinics for junior level, high school and college coaches. We have produced three highly regarded instructional videotapes, and we are now examining other ways to share NFL coaches' insights with youth, high school and college coaches around the country.

These tools are just the early fruits of the NFLCA's commitment to educating young football players, their parents and their coaches. As coaches, we know that from quality instruction comes quality play. From quality play comes enjoyment, self-worth and confidence. We see it in the eyes of the young men we coach every day. With this and the increasingly broad line of NFLCA products and services now available, we're certain that we'll being seeing that look in the eyes of more happily determined kids for years to come.

Larry Kennan
Executive Director
National Football League Coaches Association
Washington, DC

Introduction

I n our careers as strength training and conditioning coaches, we have worked very closely with some of the best athletes in the world. In many cases, the reason these athletes made the leap from "good" to "great" was their commitment to conditioning. Football success is based on a lot of factors, such as instinct, toughness, team spirit, intelligence, speed and strength. But none of these characteristics is worth much unless the body is finely tuned. This tuning, or conditioning, not only allows the body to perform at peak efficiency but it helps that athlete endure the physicality of the game.

During my years with the Detroit Lions and Steve's years with the Tennessee Titans, we have seen conditioning make an enormous difference in athletes' careers. It helped them avoid injury and recover more quickly from injuries. It helped with their basic skills such as running and jumping. It helped boost both their on-the-field confidence and their off-the field sense of well-being. It also helped maintain their health beyond their playing days. This book is intended to help young football players learn how to get in football shape through conditioning, but just as importantly, it's a primer for any youngster looking to embark on a long-term program of physical conditioning.

We applaud the National Football League Coaches Association for undertaking this project, and we have no doubt that the young athletes who study this book and the other books in the NFLCA series, will grow in their athleticism, enhance their fitness, and ultimately enjoy football even more.

Good Luck.

Bert Hill
Dallas, TX
with
Steve Watterson
Nashville, TN

ChapterOne

Success through Conditioning

The average football play—from the time the ball is snapped until the whistle blows—generally lasts from two to five seconds. That sounds like a short interval, but it can be deceiving because football plays are so intense. The time between plays depends upon the level that you are playing, but it's going to be anywhere from thirty to forty-five seconds.

▲ The time between football plays is only thirty to forty-five seconds. Get prepared with conditioning.

Then it's time for another play. This makes football and the conditioning for football different from, say, soccer, which requires constant jogging punctuated by sprints. This book will teach conditioning while incorporating characteristics that are unique to football.

Our goal is to get you in top football condition so you can perform at the highest level possible. If you look at the way a game flows, an eight- or ten-play drive is pretty significant. You very seldom see drives that last longer than that. So if you are out there for eight or ten plays, you come off the field and get a two- to four-minute break. If you are playing both ways you get no break. Then you go back out and do it all over again. That doesn't necessarily mean that you start your program at the highest intensity level. You should start your program at a lower intensity, working for anywhere from thirty to sixty seconds during lower intensity drills to help develop the energy system and the recovery system to perform at that level.

Imagine running sixty 40-yard dashes—4.8 or 4.9 seconds each—with a forty-second rest in between each one. That's how demanding and tiring the game of football can be. Once you become physically tired you'll have a very difficult time focusing on and reacting to what's going on during the course of a game. So if you're talking about playing at a high level—regardless of whether it's junior high school, high school, or college—you have to be able to think, focus, and react to what's going on around you. If you're not in top physical condition you're not going to be able to think, react, and focus in the fourth quarter, when the game is usually decided.

As this conditioning program unfolds, you will get gradually closer to actual game situations. So you will have drills where you run for two to five seconds with change of direction and acceleration. Think about it: If you are not prepared, the simple act of getting into and out of a three-point stance sixty or seventy times can be draining. If you play defensive line or offensive line and don't do drill work that requires you to get in or out of your stance, you are in for a rude awakening when practices and games come around.

▲ **If you're not in top physical condition, you're not going to be able to think, react, and focus.**

On top of all that, add the weight of your pads, helmet, cleats, and uniform. You can simulate the weight of the equipment on your body. You should weigh your shoulder pads, helmet, jersey, etc., to see how much they weigh (usually anywhere from six to twelve pounds) and then put on a weighted vest during conditioning workouts to simulate this added weight. Start with four pounds then add a pound or two each week until you are up to your equipment weight.

One coaching method used to be to start off the season with two-a-day practices (a practice in the morning and another in the afternoon). The players spent all summer getting ready for these brutal all-day sessions. On about the third day of two-a-days, the coaches would start wondering why a group of fifty or sixty well-conditioned young men would sud-

> **. . . proper conditioning allows you to play all out on every single play.**

denly begin moving sluggishly through wind sprints and other drills. Ultimately they realized that as hard as their players had trained all summer, all they wore for those workouts was shorts and a T-shirt. Suddenly they were loaded down with anywhere from eight to twelve pounds of equipment, running around in the hot sun for two practices a day, three days in a row.

It all comes back to preparing yourself specifically for the activity that's coming up. If you don't have access to a weighted vest then put your pads on and get out and do your drill work with pads on because that's another factor that comes into play. Football generally starts in the summertime. In the summer months most places in the United States are pretty warm. If you have not prepared yourself for getting in and out of your stance, running sprints and changing directions then you're going to struggle.

Ultimately, proper conditioning allows you to play all out on every single play. That's critical because regardless of your level of play, no one ever knows what play is going to be "The Big Play." Generally, there're going to be two or three plays that determine the outcome. You want to prepare so you can wear your opponent down and win the game in the fourth quarter.

This book and DVD is about getting your body in shape for the rigors of football. But when we talk about conditioning a body for football, we're really talking about preparing your muscles and your heart/lungs. Together, the muscles of the human body (collectively known as the musculature) and the heart and lungs (referred to as the cardio-pulmonary system) are largely

> **. . . the athlete who takes some time to get to know the human body. . . will appreciate and understand his own body better . . .**

taken for granted. We move a leg or an arm, even smile or laugh, hardly aware that our muscles are doing all the work. Even more importantly, our hearts beat for our entire lives (by the way, the heart itself is a muscle), and our lungs supply our bodies with oxygen without our even having to think of it.

It is possible to get into top football condition without knowing how the body works. However, the athlete who takes some time to get to know the human body—how it functions, its capabilities, and its limits—will appreciate and understand his own body better, and therefore become a better steward of his body and a better athlete.

Understanding Muscles

The human body has 650 muscles, which account for roughly half of the average person's weight. Even though there are three basic types of muscle, they are made of the same material—hundreds or thousands of elastic fibers (depending on the size of the muscle in question). Their job is to turn energy into motion.

There are three types of muscle in the human body: *Skeletal, Smooth, and Cardiac.*

Skeletal muscles (also known as voluntary muscles or striated muscles) are the ones we can see and feel on our own bodies. Of the three types of muscle they are the ones most closely associated with strength and athletic performance. Take the large bicep of an NFL player, that's a skeletal muscle. See the large thighs on an Olympic weightlifter, those are skeletal muscles. If you've ever pursued a weight-training regimen, the muscles you are working on are skeletal muscles.

Skeletal muscles are given their name because they are attached directly to the bones of the skeletal system. The term "striated" is often used to describe them because skeletal muscles with their alternating dark and light fibers appear to be striped. These muscles come in pairs: one muscle is designed to move a certain bone in one direction, and the companion muscle is designed to move that bone back. These muscles move voluntarily, meaning that they move only when the athlete sends a message from his brain to the nervous system of the body instructing the nervous system to move a certain muscle. The nerve then stimulates that particular muscle to contract or relax. The conditioning exercises in this book are by and large targeted at skeletal muscles.

Smooth muscles (also known as involuntary muscles) are largely responsible for managing internal bodily functions. For instance the human digestive tract, blood vessels, bladder and diaphragm are largely controlled by smooth muscle. These "involuntary" muscles do not require a person's conscious decision in order to be activated; they function on their own and on an as-needed basis. For instance, if we had to make a conscious decision to take every breath, we would suffocate during our sleep. But the involuntary muscles in our bodies see to these vital functions for us.

The *Cardiac* muscles (Myocardium) refer to the heart, the most important muscle in the entire human body. It's also the busiest, pumping blood throughout your body twenty-four hours a day for your entire life. Like smooth muscle, cardiac muscle functions on its own. Under stress it is told by the brain and nervous system to pump faster or slower, but it functions independently.

While the heart can gain from conditioning and exercise, it's really the skeletal muscles that allow an athlete to perform in his sport. During a typical football game, an athlete will use virtually every muscle in his body. He may use the small muscles attached to his eyes to scan the field for defenders. But the muscles he needs to exercise, develop, and rely in most in a game are the skeletal variety. He'll use the muscles in his thighs (quadriceps and hamstrings) for speed, and he may use the muscles in his chest (pectorals), shoulders (deltoid), and arms (biceps) to fend off blockers.

As we said earlier, skeletal muscles are "attached" to bones (the muscle is not directly attached to the bone; instead it is attached to a tendon which in turn is attached to the bone). The basic action of any muscle is contraction. For example, when you think about moving your arm, your brain sends a signal down a nerve cell telling your biceps muscle to contract. When a muscle gets a signal from the brain to contract, it does so, moving the tendon and then the tendon moves the bone. Tendons are very strong and can endure enormous stresses. Occasionally, however, tendons get torn. In such cases the tendon has been pulled off of or partially pulled off of the bone. These injuries can be prevented with a thorough stretching and warm-up period prior to any conditioning, weight training, or athletic exercise.

Training for the Real Thing

What has happened over time—particularly over the last twenty years with all the advances in health sciences—is that owners, management, and coaches have become more educated about the value and importance of conditioning. They have also come to an understanding about the importance of specificity of training (specific to the game and specific to position). Today, the exercises in a football player's conditioning regimen far more closely resemble the on-the-field game than did the exercises of thirty or forty years ago. That is a theme you will find throughout this book.

The conditioning program detailed here is not unlike a football practice. If you watch professional, college, or even high school teams practice, they generally break their practices into segments where they perform fundamental activities that occur during the game such as blocking drills, one-on-one tackling drills, tip drills, and fumble recovery drills. You'll do the same thing, but instead of having one complex drill where, say, you have to begin from a dead start, accelerate, hit somebody, and then make a tackle, you'll break that sequence down into several independent drills. At first, you'll just work on your start. Then you'll come back and work on another drill that might involve the physical activity of hitting somebody or making the tackle. Then, as you get closer and closer to game day, you make the drills or activities as close to actual game conditions as possible.

> *Another important area where conditioning can really help you is change of direction or agility.*

Another important area where conditioning can really help you is change of direction or agility. As you probably know, football is not a game of straight lines. A football player is constantly changing direction—forward to back, side to side—whatever it might be. Very seldom do you see a football player run a straight line for twenty or thirty yards. Unless it's a kick return or a deep pass pattern, there is almost always going to be some change of direction involved. To prepare for this, you can run a lot of different drills in which there are orange construction-type cones indicating where you're going to make a change of direction. After you've used a particular layout of cones for a while, have a coach or friend change the pattern so you don't know exactly when the change of direction is going to occur. Or you can run until your coach or teammate gives you a visual cue to change direction, simulating the way it would happen in a game.

While this book is designed for football conditioning, that doesn't mean that this will only help those who are actively playing football. Anyone who's interested in getting in terrific condition can benefit. A lot of football coaches—guys who no longer play the game—still follow their teams' workouts. Even though their playing days are behind them, they know the value of these programs and exercises when it comes to staying in shape.

Note: Before you play football or attempt any of the exercises listed in this book—or any book, for that matter—make sure you talk about it with your doctor. Only a doctor can tell you if your body is ready for the demands of the game and the conditioning regimen offered here. It's also critical to practice the following exercises using proper form and technique. On the DVD included with this book, correct form and technique are discussed and demonstrated by professionals. Please review it to ensure that you are employing proper, effective techniques.

Surviving the Fourth Quarter

The ultimate objective in conditioning for football is to have yourself physically prepared to play in a football game. In a typical game, a team is going to average anywhere from sixty to sixty-five plays on offense and about the same number on defense. If you play both offense and defense—as many high school players do—that's about 130 plays per game. So you should be prepared to go out and perform for four quarters and still have a little gas in the tank at the end of the game. As you may know, at the professional level the majority of games are decided by three points or less, and the deciding play almost always takes place in the fourth quarter. So you've got to be in good condition and ready to excel throughout the game but particularly in those last three minutes of the fourth quarter.

The bottom line is that you need a total program that is balanced. Early in your program you may want to place more emphasis on strength training and sacrifice a little bit when it comes to conditioning. As time progresses and you get closer to the game, there should be less emphasis on strength training and more focus on your conditioning. That's because the number one factor in playing well during a game is being in good enough condition to do all the specific tasks that are required.

Of course, good conditioning not only helps on the field and in practice, but it can also help in the weight room. It complements a strength-training program. Good conditioning allows you to recover faster between sets in the weight room and affords you more endurance for your entire workout.

ChapterTwo
Conditioning vs. Strength

Improving strength and conditioning both take dedication, both improve your health and performance, and both belong in a conscientious football player's overall plan for excellence. But as much as strength work and conditioning work have in common, it's important and useful to know the differences between them.

When you combine all the elements of football-specific

▲ While building strength is important, conditioning can prepare you for the hits, running, twists and direction changes of football.

strength training and football-specific conditioning you have a well-rounded program that prepares you to play this unique game. You may have heard certain sports described as contact sports. For instance, basketball and soccer are defined as contact sports because they require frequent physical contact. But football is more than a contact sport—it's a game of outright collisions. If you plan to play football, your overall plan must prepare your body for the collisions that are inevitably going to take place. Ideally, you want to combine a three-day-a-week conditioning program such as the one in this book with a three-day-a-week strength program. For more information on strength training, read the NFLCA book, *How to Get in Football Shape: Strength Training*.

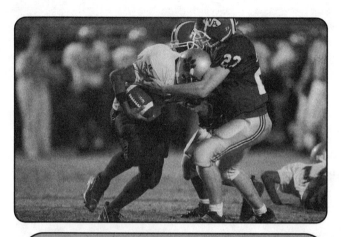

▲ Drills will help you prepare your body for the actual game.

In addition to building strength, you need to prepare your body to withstand not only the hits but also the running, agility, twists, changes of direction and all the other physical stresses that take place throughout the course of a football game.

This book and DVD will help you get in shape in just six weeks. The program contains a series of activities and drills that mimic what occurs in a football game. That way you can prepare for the game at a lower intensity level than the actual game requires, but the motions you are performing are directly related. What you're really trying to do is take the game, analyze what is occurring during that game, and then craft drills that will help prepare your body to function at 100 percent from kickoff through the fourth quarter. In basic terms, conditioning is getting the body in shape. In practical terms, you're helping prevent your body from getting tired because when you're tired you can't play your best. More importantly, when you're tired you are more likely to sustain an injury.

Of course, since you are playing a sport where young men are running into each other at a high rate of speed there's always going to be the possibility of injury. Experience has shown that if you go at full speed the chances of getting injured are significantly reduced. If two guys are going full speed against each other, Newton's third law ("for every action, there is

> Ideally you will com- ▶
> bine a 3-day-a-week
> conditioning program
> with a 3-day-a-week
> strength program.

an equal and opposite reaction")
says they should bounce off each
other, get up and go. But if
you've got one guy going full
speed and another guy going half
speed, the half speed guy is going
to absorb the blow from the full
speed guy, and generally he's the one most likely to get hurt. So you want
to try to put yourself in a position where you can play at full speed and
minimize the risk of injury. One of the best ways to minimize the risk is to
keep yourself in top physical condition.

Why Supervision Is Important

Supervision and spotting is recommendedfor any and all strength work.
This is because of the dangers inherent in lifting and moving heavy
weights. However, when it comes to conditioning work, you can largely go
out on your own if you are responsible and comfortable in doing so. The
only time when supervision really comes into play with regard to conditioning is when you are warming up or performing risky exercises.

Have a supervisor take you through the warm-up process to make sure you do it properly. This can be accomplished through solid guidance and training from your coaches, or if available, daily supervision of your warm-up period. Your actual conditioning work can generally be performed without supervision. Naturally, you need to warm up prior to stretching, and then you need to stretch properly. Once that's completed, you can be taught how to do the different drills for agility, for change in direction, for conditioning, and for speed. After that, if you have a workout partner—or even if you're on your own—you can use a stopwatch to monitor your progress or monitor the intensity at which you are performing drills.

When performing risky exercises, such as the box jumps detailed later in this book, you should always have a spotter who can protect you from a fall.

What Kind of Shape Are You In?

▲ Strength training prepares your body for the collisions of football.

If you were mapping out a trip, you would determine your starting point and your ending point. By knowing where you are, you have a better idea of where you have to go. In much the same way, conditioning requires you to measure your goals. You need to assess your level of conditioning before you begin a program and again after you have completed the program. You need some barometer—some way to measure yourself—to determine if you are below, beyond, or at whatever level of performance you are shooting for. To make sense of that barometer, it's important to start out by doing some form of self-evaluation. This way you have a baseline by which you can measure your improvement over time. Not only is this information vital to achieving your goal, but it's instrumental in feeding the motivation and the momentum that enable you to achieve your goal.

Measure Your Progress

If you are trying to develop your strength you could measure your progress easily. You would simply compare the amount of weight you are lifting now with the amount you were lifting two or three weeks ago. But conditioning isn't as cut-and-dry. How do you measure where you are and where you want to be?

One good way is *quarters,* meaning quarter mile sprints (440 yards or 400 meters). When you run them, try to cover the distance in a minute and a half to a minute and forty seconds, then take a five-minute rest and try another. If you can run four of those, each within that time frame, then you are in good shape.

If you're preparing for a football season and you want to establish your base level of conditioning, go to a nearby track, warm up thoroughly, and then run a mile. After you've completed the mile, run one time around the track and time yourself. After you have run one time around, walk a lap—taking five to six minutes to complete it—and then run one more time around the track. See how close that second lap time is to your first lap time. That will give you a reliable barometer of where you are conditioning-wise. Write those numbers down. After you have gone through a conditioning program for six weeks, come back and test yourself again. With proper conditioning, the difference between those two times should narrow significantly. Keeping a conditioning journal is very helpful for tracking your progress. Get into the practice of keeping a journal by using the one included in the back of this book.

ChapterThree
Getting Started

The Functional Warm-Up

The philosophy with regards to warming up has changed over time. It used to be that players would just go out on the football field, stretch for five or ten minutes, and then go right into practice. But in  recent years it has become apparent through research that it's vitally important to warm up properly and thoroughly. In the past, players didn't warm up in the same way that we think of warming up today. Instead, they started with stretching exercises. However, researchers have discovered that if you go through a warm-up program first, you increase the blood flow in the areas that you want to stretch, and by warming the body temperature you simultaneously loosen muscles. A great visual example is a piece of bacon. When you take bacon out of the refrigerator it really doesn't want to bend or move very much, but after you've warmed it up it's much more pliable. Our muscles are like that, too.

So it's imperative for you to go out and do a warm-up. By the way, it's also a good idea for all athletes—whether you are in high school, college or the pros—to do a little stretching at the end of every day. Players should not only stretch every day in practice but also stretch every morning and evening on their own. The extra stretching will help improve your muscles' recovery time, and the shorter recovery time will help you improve your overall flexibility.

Warm-Up Drills

As part of this program, you're going to do a series of drills, strides, and movements that will help warm up your muscles, ligaments, tendons, and your groin area—everything that comes into play in football. Basically, you're going to try to warm up these areas *functionally*. This means the warm-up mimics the game itself. It involves a series of strides, steps and other movements that are similar to the strides, steps,

> *. . . it's also a good idea for all athletes—whether you are in high school, college or the pros—to do a little stretching at the end of every day.*

and movements that you are likely to use on the field during practice or an actual game. *Note: Always start with small movements and move to wider movements as you warm up.*

You'll see on the DVD that we generally start our warm-up period with a simple jog around the field, just enough to get the blood flowing. After that, the next step is to engage in a series of warm-up strides like those that follow.

High Knee

Football teams have been using the high knee for decades. If you watch old films from training camps being run by legendary Green Bay Packers head coach Vince Lombardi, you'll see his players running through webbing that forces them to lift their knees to somewhere above their belt line. It's important to note that this is done for only fifty yards (twenty-five yards out and twenty-five yards back) and not at a high rate of speed. The high knee warms up the whole lower body and leg region.

The High Knee

Butt Kicks

This exercise is also performed at half speed. It's simply a jogging motion in which the foot that is coming off the ground is brought all the way up to the buttocks so that your heel actually makes contact with your rear end. This exercise is typically done twice for fifty yards (twenty-five yards out and twenty-five yards back). It stretches the hamstrings and the quadriceps.

Power Steps

To do power steps, spread your legs slightly wider than shoulder-width and keep your toes pointing straight downfield. Lift your right foot and move it laterally out to your right. Then, keeping your toes pointed straight ahead, use the muscles on the inside of your right thigh to pull your left leg over to your right. When you watch the DVD you'll see that this exercise is not done quickly. Repeat by moving slowly to the left. Executing this exercise properly will help you warm up the adductors and abductors in your thighs.

The Karioka

Although the karioka sounds like the name of a nightclub or a dance step, it's actually a great warm up for the lower body, the muscles in the hips, and the muscles that allow torso rotation. The karioka can be performed on any surface, but a football field is always best.

To begin, face either end zone, keeping your arms fairly relaxed. First, step sideways with your right foot. Shift your weight to your right and then

◀ pull or propel yourself with the muscles of your inner thighs (adductors). Bring the left leg towards the right, but then cross it behind. Extend your right leg to the side again and cross the left foot, this time in front. Look in the direction you are traveling but be sure to keep your feet parallel. Move quickly but not in a full-out run. Change direction, leading this time with the left foot. Start with small strides and widen them as you warm up. Be sure to keep your toes pointing forward throughout, as that will give you the greatest benefit. While the karioka isn't easy to describe on paper, it's a terrific way to warm up the hips, torso, lower body, calves, and the muscles in your feet.

Runs

Finally, finish up this functional warm-up with two twenty-five-yard runs at 75 to 80 percent takeoff speed, and you're ready for the all-important stretching period.

Stretching

Track 4

On the DVD with this book, the recommended duration of each stretching exercise is spelled out. Additionally, while the various techniques are described in this chapter, the DVD shows actual NFL players demonstrating these exercises.

In general terms, the long-term benefit of stretching is that it helps make your body more flexible from a physical perspective. There is no doubt that the more flexible you are the more easily your body will tolerate being moved into positions that it wouldn't normally be able to attain without

▲ Being flexible allows your body to move in more directions without being injured.

incurring injury. However, there are three more meaningful benefits to a conscientiously applied stretching program:

1. The more flexible you are, the quicker and more effectively you will be able to warm up.

2. Stretching allows for increased blood flow to your muscles, improving your circulation and allowing you to do more.

3. Stretching builds a base on which you can improve your endurance.

Are You Stretching Enough?

Naturally, you want to make sure that you stretch your whole body to maximize performance. In particular, you should focus on the groin area (upper inner thigh), the hamstrings (rear of the thigh), the quads (front outer thigh), the abdominal muscles (belly), the lower back, and the shoulders and neck. You should allow for anywhere from seven to ten minutes to go through a simple, static stretching program to make sure that you are loose, warmed up and ready to go on to the next step, which will be the agility program.

Note: Stretching is not something that should only be done in preparation for a game, practice, or some other physical activity. It's a good idea to stretch a couple of times a day.

As mentioned earlier, it's a good idea for players to stretch on their own time each morning and night in addition to each day in practice. As you know, a stretch prior to physical activity helps prepare you for that activity, but a stretch at night before bed helps to eliminate lactic acids from your muscles. Lactic acids are waste products that are left behind after you exercise. Stretching helps you accelerate the process of flushing these waste products from your muscles. In turn, that improves your body's

The long term benefit of stretching is that it helps make your body more flexible. . .

ability to recover from the stresses of physical activity and helps improve your flexibility.

Remember that the air temperature will affect the length of time it takes you to effectively loosen up. If you are working out in a hot environment such as Florida in August it probably won't take you very long to stretch and get loosened up. But if you are practicing in below-freezing temperatures—Green Bay, Wisconsin in January comes to mind—you will need to spend more time warming up and maybe not quite as much time in the stretching phase. As mentioned earlier, you want to warm up the muscles so that you can get them stretched out. There are no shortcuts when it comes to doing that, but it's of critical importance because it will effectively lower your risk of suffering an injury. If warming up and stretching seems like a daunting task, you can take comfort in the fact that your entire jog, warm-up, and stretching time *combined* need not take any longer than fifteen minutes.

You'll see later on that we talk about some position-specific work; however, at this point in your stretching program, you should be following a general stretching routine that works for everybody on the team. Once the functional warm-up and general stretching programs have been completed, *then* you can branch off and do position-specific work, taking an extra minute or two to stretch problem areas or address nagging injuries.

For example, wide receivers—who need to take long strides at top speed—may want to spend a little extra time stretching their hamstrings. One injury that hampers a lot of athletes, regardless of their sport or their position is a pulled hamstring. You hear more about wide receivers, defensive backs, and running backs having hamstring problems, but it affects a lot of players. However, a large percentage of hamstring pulls can be avoided with proper stretching.

How Muscles Help Each Other

You need to stretch more than the hamstring itself to prevent it from getting pulled. This proves how important a total-body stretching program can be. Even players who stretch

A professional player can keep his career alive by staying flexible.

their hamstrings several times a day can end up with hamstring problems. That's because hamstring pulls are not caused solely by tight hamstrings. They can also be caused by tight quadriceps (the large muscles on the front outer thighs). The quadriceps and hamstrings are called *antagonistic* muscles. That is, one muscle reacts to the other. Therefore, if you thoroughly stretch your quads, that will allow your hamstrings to relax, and vice-versa.

While the quadriceps muscles are not talked about as often as the hamstrings, they are the primary mover for wide receivers and defensive backs who rely on sprinting for performance. That's why it's not uncommon to find wideouts, cornerbacks, and safeties listed on NFL injury reports with a "strained quad." The quad is a hip flexor (meaning it helps your upper leg move forward and back from the hip) and also partly functions as a knee extensor (meaning it helps the lower leg move forward from the knee). In order for that extension to take place, the hamstring has to relax. It can only relax if it's allowed to by having enough flexibility in the quadriceps. With most hamstring pulls, what's really missing is flexibility of the quadriceps.

One final note before you go through the list of flexibility exercises. Whenever you are instructed to "hold" a stretching position, that means you should hold still in that position until ten seconds have elapsed. As players are sometimes told, "You're born loose, you die stiff." A professional player can help keep his career alive by staying flexible.

Flexibility Exercises (Standing)
Roll Neck ▼

This is a simple exercise for one of the most important parts of the body (at least as far as football is concerned). Standing straight up with your arms at your sides, simply place your chin near your chest and in a slow, smooth, controlled manner move your head in a circular motion. Here's the sequence you should be following: Chin to chest, left ear toward left shoulder, arched neck, right ear toward right shoulder, chin to chest. Then repeat the exercise in the opposite direction.

Roll Hip

Begin in a standing position. Place your hands on your hips and rotate your midsection, moving your hips forward, to the left, the rear, to the right, and forward again. Then repeat the motion going in the opposite direction. This should not look or feel like a series of moves, but instead it should come across like one smooth sweeping motion.

Windmill

Again, begin in a standing position. Keeping your feet planted, simply rotate your torso so that your right arm swings around in front of you and ends up pointing left. At the same time, your left arm swings behind you and points toward your right. Reverse and repeat. There should be no jerky motions here, just smooth rotations back and forth. This gives you a full range of motion, works the SI (Sacroiliac) joint, your thoracic region (chest), your spiny muscles, and your hips.

Shoulder Rolls ▼

As you'd expect, shoulder rolls help you loosen your shoulder area. Start in a standing position with your hands at your sides. Simultaneously swing both arms forward, up and behind you in a circular motion. Then reverse direction and repeat. This exercise can also be performed one arm at a time.

After these four standing exercises, you are ready to move on to some seated exercises.

Flexibility Exercises (Seated)
Hamstring/Calf Stretch

◀ While sitting down on the ground, spread your legs wide and keep your toes pointing straight up and perhaps even slightly back. Slowly lean your chest toward the ground in front of you and stretch your arms out equidistant between your feet. This will stretch your hamstrings and your calves. Be sure to keep your toes up or you will not get the full benefit of this exercise. *Hold.*

From the same sitting/legs spread position, move your chest down towards your right knee and grasp your right foot with both hands. If you are not flexible enough to grasp your foot the first time you attempt this stretch don't worry. Over time you will become more flexible. Be aware that many athletes try simply to move their head toward the knee, but the full benefit to the gluteus muscles (the buttocks) and the hamstring comes from moving the chest slowly toward the knee and grasping the feet. This works your hip, gluteus, and hamstring. *Hold.*

Switch and do the same exercise with your left leg and foot. Then place your legs straight out in front of you with your feet together. Lean forward and grasp your feet. *Hold.*

Modified Hurdler

If you've ever watched or been involved in track and field you've likely seen or performed the hurdler. Traditionally, the hurdler stretch is done from a sitting position with one leg  extended straight out in front and the other leg bent at the knee, with the foot positioned near the buttock. While this technique is useful for runners, research has shown that it can irritate the knees of athletes competing in com-

The Modified Hurdler

pact sports. As a result, football players are taught to do this stretch differently.

Still sitting, place your left leg straight out in front of you. Then bend your right leg so that the sole of your right foot is flush against your left knee or calf. Reach out for your left foot. *Hold*. Then repeat the exercise on your other leg.

Cradle

Still sitting, and with your right leg extended, put your left hand under your left knee and around the ankle or instep of your left foot. Cradle the leg and swing your torso gently from side to side. Then switch legs. This is a great workout for your hips, adductors, and glutes.

◄ Step Over

From the seated cradle position described above, simply take your right foot and place it outside your left knee. Using your right elbow (or a hug with both arms for tight-hipped individuals) keep the right leg in place and turn your torso to the right. *Hold.* Then switch legs.

Butterfly ▼

From a seated position place the soles of your feet together as close to the inner thigh as possible. Place your elbows on your inner thighs, tuck the head down, and place moderate pressure on your thighs with your elbows. *Hold.* This not only works both inner thighs but also helps stretch the back and neck as well.

Low-Back Stretch

Lie on your back in a spread eagle ▶ position. Put your right leg across your body and your right foot into your left hand. *Hold.* Then switch legs. The key here is to keep both of your shoulders on the ground. If this exercise is done correctly, you will feel it in your chest and lower back.

◀ Rocking Roll

From a seated position, pull your legs up to your chest to form a human ball. Keep your arms on your shins to maintain that round shape and gently rock and roll on your back, rolling up to the base of the neck and back down to your buttocks. Do not roll so high up that you place pressure on the neck itself, as a neck injury may result. A simple, short rocking motion is all that's needed to work your back from the cervical region to the lumbar region.

Switch to a kneeling position. Place your hands on your ankles and try to lift your hips up and out. This stretches both your abs and your glutes. *Hold.*

Hip Drops

Keep your left knee on the ground and put your right foot on the ground in front of you—the classic "take a knee" position. Keeping your back perpendicular to the field, lower your hips toward

The Rocking Roll
(in kneeling position)

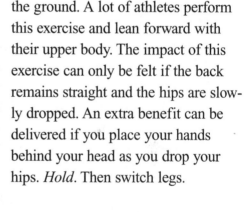

Hip Drops

the ground. A lot of athletes perform this exercise and lean forward with their upper body. The impact of this exercise can only be felt if the back remains straight and the hips are slowly dropped. An extra benefit can be delivered if you place your hands behind your head as you drop your hips. *Hold.* Then switch legs.

With your left knee on the ground, extend your right leg directly in front of you, keeping your right heel on the ground and your toes pointing up. Reach and grasp your right foot with both hands. *Hold.* Then switch legs.

◀ Wide Straddle

Stand up. Place your feet as far apart as you can while bending over from the hips. Reach out to touch the ground in front of you. Those of you who are exceptionally flexible might be able to put your hands around your ankles from the inside.

In the same position—wide base, bending from the waist—reach to your left foot with both hands. *Hold.* Then reach to the right foot with both hands.

Next, squat down with most of your weight over your right foot. Extend the left leg out to your left with your toes pointing directly downfield. *Hold.* Repeat the same sequence with your right leg.

Finally, squat down low. Place your hands near one another on the ground and use your elbows to apply outward pressure on your legs.

Legs and Ankles

One area that is highly over-looked among athletes and their coaches is ankle flexibility. Your foot is your anchor. That is what you are going to be basing your entire body weight and momen-tum on.

Ankle flexibility is vital for maintaining balance. In order for you to achieve and maintain a low center of gravity and to put yourself in a position that will

▲ Ankle flexibility is vital for maintaining balance. Ankles are the base for your entire body weight.

allow you to move, react, and hit, you need to bend at the ankle. Your ankles allow your knees to come forward. Watch any good linebacker in college or in the NFL, and their ankles are almost constantly flexed with their knees out over their feet. If you have poor ankle flexibility and try to get yourself in a low-center-of-gravity position, you will end up bending over at the waist with your legs staying fairly straight. That's a very difficult position in which to move and maintain any type of agility or balance. That also means you become an easy target for a defender. Good ankle flexibility and good quad flexibility will allow you to get in a low position, keeping your body weight centered. You'll enjoy much better agility.

ChapterFour
Speed

After the functional warm-up and stretching, the next factor you need to consider is speed. Speed may be the single most important characteristic for success in football, regardless of age group. The biggest difference you see among players at all

▲ Speed may be the single most important characteristic for success in football.

ages and playing levels is the speed at which things happen—the speed at which the players are able to move.

The speed at which the NFL game is played is astounding. As you move away from the sideline, to the stands, and then to your living room, the speed of the game seems to slow down, but believe me, it is very fast. There is no doubt that—regardless of position, regardless of the level—speed separates good players from great players.

Speed is not only a vital asset for a successful football player, it can also make up for a lot of other weaknesses. For instance, speed can overcome bad coaching. It can overcome mistakes by giving you the ability to make up ground. So in any conditioning program, you want to put an emphasis on improving speed. That means looking at your current running technique and improving upon it so that you are able to move faster.

Speed reveals itself in several ways. The first is acceleration—how fast you can go from standing still to full speed. Let's relate that specifically to football. Most plays—98 percent—are going to last for between two and five seconds. Most of the action on those plays will take place within ten yards of the line of scrimmage. So if it takes you forty yards and eight or nine seconds to get to full speed, that's not good enough. Football requires that you get to full speed quickly.

As you may know, there are two ways to measure speed: pure speed and game speed. When coaches talk about how fast a player is you normally hear them say things such as, "He runs a 4.6 forty." That means the player can run forty yards in 4.6 seconds coming out of three-point stance. That's called pure speed—an all-out sprint with only speed in mind. While pure speed is a valuable and useful indicator, it's not as valuable or as meaning-

▲ Game speed measures how fast a player runs while actually playing against an opposing team.

ful as game speed. Game speed is how fast a player runs when he is actually playing in a game, under the stress of an opposition, with a play he has to execute, and with the added responsibility, perhaps, of holding onto the ball. Very often players who don't have very good pure speed will have very good game speed.

There are a lot of factors that dictate both pure and

game speed. First, how well do you carry your equipment? From time to time, you'll see players who can run fast in shorts, but when you put eight to ten pounds of equipment on them, they don't play very fast. Other players—particularly younger players—may have outstanding pure speed, but when they get out on the field they can get overwhelmed by all that's going on around them. That slows down their game speed.

Here's a great example of the value that coaches place on pure speed vs. game speed. There was a player named Jamie Watson. Jamie's football coach at Jefferson Davis High School in Montgomery, Alabama, was Billy Livins. During his senior year, Jamie was being recruited by Southern Mississippi. One day, one of the Southern Miss. coaches called Coach Livins and said, "Coach, what kind of forty time does Jamie run?" Coach Livins sounded stunned: "Forty time? I've got five or six guys that run good forties. I thought you

> **Coaches talk about speed all the time, but. . . different coaches are looking for different kinds of speed.**

were looking for a football player." Coaches talk about speed all the time, but whatever level you look at you're going to find that different coaches are looking for different types of speed. One coach may be looking for a guy who's a good football player and plays at a high speed because he knows the game, he anticipates, he can react and he has worked on his agility. Another may be looking for a guy who can run down the track in a hurry, even though he doesn't really know how to carry that onto the field.

Another example is former Detroit Lions great, Barry Sanders. Coming out of high school, Barry weighed about 170 pounds soaking wet and, as hard as it is to believe now, there weren't a lot of colleges that were recruiting him. His greatest asset as a player was his legs. One of the things that led to his success was the tutelage of a strength coach named John Stucky at Oklahoma State. Stucky—who later went on to the University of Tennessee—had Barry do a lot of hang cleans and squats, both of which focus on various speed-enhancing leg muscles. Barry felt that those two exercises laid the foundation for him to develop the change of direction, agility, and acceleration qualities that he enjoyed in the NFL.

As you may know, Barry had the quickest acceleration you'll ever see and some of the most unbelievable agility. His ability to step, to sidestep and move laterally, to back up, and to go forward was incredible. On the stopwatch he might have run a 4.5 forty-yard dash, but on the field, once he hit the hole, nobody ever caught him. After he was through the hole he was ten or fifteen yards down the field before anybody even knew he had the football. That's game speed.

Chris Spielman was a linebacker from Ohio State who also played for the Detroit Lions. He always kept himself in good shape but did not have tremendous speed; however, he worked on being able to react and move and accelerate to the point of attack. That ability—not his pure speed—enabled Chris to stay in the NFL and have the type of career that he had. In ten seasons with Detroit and the Buffalo Bills he had 936 tackles, 427 assists, 11 sacks and 6 interceptions.

> *. . . if some of the greatest players of all time had size, strength, or speed deficiencies and overcame them, then maybe you can too.*

The bottom line is that if some of the greatest players of all time had size, strength, or speed deficiencies and overcame them, then maybe you can too. Someone out there playing high school football may very well be the next Barry Sanders if he commits himself to a training regimen, puts his time in, and works at it on a daily basis. How far you go is up to you.

Improving Speed

There are four main factors that determine running speed: *Strength, flexibility, mechanics,* and *relaxation.* These four factors all come together to some extent in sprint training.

Strength can occur naturally, but more often than not it's a result of a conscientious weight-training program. (See *How to Get in Football Shape: Strength Training.*)

Flexibility has already been discussed at length previously in this book. Review the "Stretching" section that begins on p. 20.

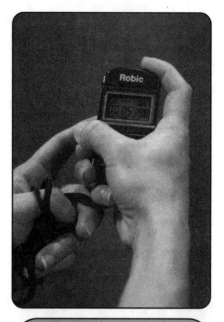

▲ Speed is determined by strength, flexibility, mechanics, and relaxation.

Mechanics is another way of saying technique. Specifically you look at the body position and the position of the foot when that particular leg is in the "unsupported phase" or in the air. When, say, your right leg is off the ground, what is the angle formed by your right foot and ankle? You would like to have that foot flexed upward so that the bottom of the foot—the sole of the shoe—is parallel with the ground. The feeling is that you are pulling your toes up when your leg is in an unsupported phase. In his heyday with the San Francisco 49ers, All-Pro running back Roger Craig had this technique down to an art. This allows you to cycle the leg through so when the foot comes down and hits the turf it will plant slightly behind the center of gravity, which is going to keep you moving forward.

If you let that foot drop and you end up planting the foot slightly *in front* of the center of gravity, that will slow you down.

A lot of young athletes are concerned with length of stride as a factor in improving speed. Stride is the amount of ground you can cover in one running step. Fascination with stride is understandable when you see how much ground an NFL receiver or Olympic sprinter can cover in one stride. Remarkable as receivers or sprinters can be, they don't usually devote any serious time specifically to lengthening stride. Sure a long stride is nice, but it is an end, not a means. That is, stride length will improve as your mechanics improve and as your running speed improves. So rather than focus on it, think of it as a positive by-product of your overall conditioning and speed work.

Relaxation

HIGH KNEES

▲ Speed work done one-on-one with a coach works well. Otherwise a player may focus too much on beating the guy next to him.

The term "running relaxed" sounds like a contradiction in terms, but it's actually a terrific way to achieve your greatest speed potential. You want to train to run in total relaxation. Now, when a coach tells you to run hard, you probably unconsciously tighten up. For most people, the mental image associated with running hard features tightly clenched fists and a strained face. That's a problem, because the more muscles you contract when you're running, the slower you actually run. Your muscles have to relax if you are going to run your fastest.

So when developing your speed, try to emphasize relaxation. When you remove the old mental image of tension, replace it with a mental picture of relaxation and reinforce that with proper running mechanics. It's amazing how quickly you can improve. You will actually run fastest when you stop trying to run hard.

Speed is a very personal, very mental attribute. That's why dedicated speed work done one-on-one with a coach works well. Oftentimes, if you put a player in a competitive situation with another player, important things like relaxation and focus on technique go right out the window. Instead, all he's going to do is try to beat the guy next to him.

Admittedly, running relaxed does not come naturally to everyone; it almost always has to be taught. But with a little work, that concept will carry over to on-the-field performance, and you will learn how to run relaxed right up to the moment of impact. At that point you need to flex and tighten the areas of your body that need to be flexed and tightened so that you can deliver a blow to your tackler or other defender.

Metabolic Speed Program

A metabolic speed program is designed to simulate the running requirements of an actual football game. That is, the running done in the course of a game by a quarterback is vastly different from the running done by a receiver or a tight end. So this program is designed not simply to increase speed but also to increase position-specific speed.

▲ The metabolic speed program is easier with a friend. They can run the stopwatch and mark the places for you to run to.

How It Works

The program is divided up into quarters. The goal is for you to complete a minimum of three-quarters of this position-specific program. In order to get the full effect you should go as fast as possible on each run. One of the best aspects of the program is that you can cover the distances suggested in any direction. This way you can not only simulate straight-ahead speed but also movements that are characteristic of and specific to your position. For instance, wide receivers can run particular patterns for distances suggested. Offensive guards can pull or pass protect. Linebackers and defensive backs can work on drops. Offensive backs can run sweeps, slants, or pass patterns.

It is important to go all out on each exercise and only rest as outlined. During your training, keep track of your times for each quarter as well as your total exercise time. Use your journal for this. As you become better conditioned, the quarter times and total time should decrease. This program can be run alone, but it will be easier if you have a friend, coach or team- mate who can run a stopwatch and mark the spot(s) you have to run to. Again, strive to run every yard of the routine and rest precisely the number of minutes allotted.

First, mark off a fifty-yard area or use an actual football field. The per- son helping you will go to the spot you are to run to and tell you when to start. Once you cross the line you're running for, he will start the 15-second rest time. While you rest, he will move to the next yard marker. As your fif- teen-second rest period comes to an end, he will count "three-two-one" and you are on your way. The procedure continues until at least the first twenty- six exercise runs are completed. These twenty-six runs will constitute the first Quarter of your workout. You will wait three minutes and repeat all twenty-six runs again. Then at halftime, you will rest five minutes and then go through the third quarter and eventually the fourth quarter. In the begin- ning you may find it difficult to complete two quarters, but you should start with two quarters and progress to four quarters.

The next page begins the metabolic speed program with metabolic endurance sprints. We'll start with Offensive Backs.

Metabolic Endurance Sprints

Offensive Backs (QBs, Fullbacks, Running Backs)

	Distance (Yds.)	Rest Time (Secs.)
1.	7	15
2.	14	15
3.	7	15
4.	8	15
5.	5	15
6.	40	15
7.	40	15
8.	5	15
9.	2	15
10.	50	15

REST 3 MINUTES

	Distance (Yds.)	Rest Time (Secs.)
1.	5	15
2.	12	15
3.	40	15
4.	3	15
5.	40	15
6.	12	15
7.	5	15
8.	5	15
9.	15	15
10.	40	15

Metabolic Endurance Sprints

REST 3 MINUTES

	Distance (Yds.)	Rest Time (Secs.)
1.	2	15
2.	8	15
3.	40	15
4.	50	15
5.	12	15
6.	5	15

You have completed the first Quarter. Rest three minutes and repeat the above as your second Quarter. At halftime take a five-minute rest and repeat the procedure for quarters three and four.

Metabolic Endurance Sprints

Receivers (Wide Receivers, Tight Ends)

	Distance (Yds.)	Rest Time (Secs.)
1.	20	15
2.	40	15
3.	12	15
4.	30	15
5.	4	15
6.	40	15
7.	20	15
8.	10	15
9.	25	15
10.	50	15

REST 3 MINUTES

	Distance (Yds.)	Rest Time (Secs.)
1.	25	15
2.	30	15
3.	40	15
4.	12	15
5.	40	15
6.	25	15
7.	14	15
8.	7	15
9.	40	15
10.	7	15

Metabolic Endurance Sprints

REST 3 MINUTES

	Distance (Yds.)	Rest Time (Secs.)
1.	7	15
2.	40	15
3.	12	15
4.	15	15
5.	15	15
6.	40	15

You have completed the first Quarter. Rest three minutes and repeat the above as your second Quarter. At halftime take a five-minute rest and repeat the procedure for quarters three and four.

Metabolic Endurance Sprints

Defensive Backs
(Cornerbacks, Free Safeties, Strong Safeties)

	Distance (Yds.)	Rest Time (Secs.)
1.	15	15
2.	7	15
3.	3	15
4.	40	15
5.	30	15
6.	40	15
7.	4	15
8.	8	15
9.	11	15
10.	50	15

REST 3 MINUTES

	Distance (Yds.)	Rest Time (Secs.)
1.	4	15
2.	5	15
3.	23	15
4.	40	15
5.	13	15
6.	5	15
7.	8	15
8.	20	15
9.	50	15
10.	15	15

Metabolic Endurance Sprints

REST 3 MINUTES

	Distance (Yds.)	Rest Time (Secs.)
1.	7	15
2.	3	15
3.	40	15
4.	15	15
5.	30	15
6.	25	15

You have completed the first Quarter. Rest three minutes and repeat the above as your second Quarter. At halftime take a five-minute rest and repeat the procedure for quarters three and four.

Metabolic Endurance Sprints

Linebackers (Middle, Outside)

	Distance (Yds.)	Rest Time (Secs.)
1.	4	15
2.	40	15
3.	4	15
4.	5	15
5.	22	15
6.	40	15
7.	8	15
8.	3	15
9.	10	15
10.	50	15

REST 3 MINUTES

	Distance (Yds.)	Rest Time (Secs.)
1.	5	15
2.	8	15
3.	40	15
4.	40	15
5.	14	15
6.	8	15
7.	3	15
8.	30	15
9.	50	15
10.	4	15

Metabolic Endurance Sprints

REST 3 MINUTES

	Distance (Yds.)	Rest Time (Secs.)
1.	3	15
2.	40	15
3.	5	15
4.	22	15
5.	14	15
6.	40	15

You have completed the first Quarter. Rest three minutes and repeat the above as your second Quarter. At halftime take a five-minute rest and repeat the procedure for quarters three and four.

Metabolic Endurance Sprints

Defensive Line and Offensive Line

	Distance (Yds.)	Rest Time (Secs.)
1.	5	15
2.	40	15
3.	4	15
4.	2	15
5.	24	15
6.	40	15
7.	7	15
8.	4	15
9.	4	15
10.	50	15

REST 3 MINUTES

	Distance (Yds.)	Rest Time (Secs.)
1.	10	15
2.	5	15
3.	7	15
4.	40	15
5.	8	15
6.	5	15
7.	9	15
8.	18	15
9.	18	15
10.	5	15

Metabolic Endurance Sprints

REST 3 MINUTES

	Distance (Yds.)	Rest Time (Secs.)
1.	8	15
2.	4	15
3.	40	15
4.	2	15
5.	24	15
6.	15	15

You have completed the first Quarter. Rest three minutes and repeat the above as your second Quarter. At halftime take a five-minute rest and repeat the procedure for quarters three and four.

ChapterFive
Agility

Y ou hear the word *agility* a lot, but what does it really mean? For football purposes, agility is "the ability to change direction without hesitation and with a minimal loss of speed." For example, if you're a defensive player and shuffling to your right and all of a sudden you need to stop and go back to your left, you need that change of direction to occur quickly and smoothly or the runner will breeze by you.

Agility means that the movement occurs "right now" instead of a second or two from now, which would leave way too much time for your opponent to defeat you. So what you're trying to accomplish in agility drills is to make yourself more fluid.

Improve with Practice

There are specific techniques that you can practice that will allow you to anticipate which direction you need to go and also allow you to put your body in the right position to make a change in direction.

For instance, if you are shuffling across the line of scrimmage, you need to do so in a position of balance. That means that rather than shuffle with both feet close together (it's easy to be knocked over from a narrow stance), you keep your feet at shoulder width as you are shuffling. That will allow you—if you need to change direction—to stick your foot down on the ground and move. In a wide stance, your center of gravity will allow you to push off and go to the left. It's the same with backpedaling or running forward. If you are a defensive back and working on your backpedal drills (discussed later in this chapter), you've got to be able to stick your foot in the ground behind you and push off to go in a forward direction.

What you're looking for is how quickly you can stop movement in one direction and transfer that movement to another direction. That's important for every player on a football team. It can have an enormous impact on team speed and pursuit.

Off-Season Work

Your off-season program would be incomplete if it did not include some agility work. Racquetball, handball, basketball and tennis are excellent off-season activities for the football player since they force you to make many of the same kinds of moves and maintain the same kind of body control that you need in football. During the off-season you should try to participate in these types of activities at least three times a week. As the season approaches you should add to your running workouts some agility drills that force you to mirror the same kind of activities you will be doing in camp.

One drill called *ball reaction* instructs athletes to shuffle in one direction. On the fourth step, they'll plant their outside foot and reverse direction. They will practice this maneuver to both the left and right side. Then later, instead of changing direction on the fourth step, they will change direction on a cue from the coach that might arise at any time. This drill will help you learn how to move your body very quickly while maintaining a balanced position that will allow you to change direction and go back as soon as you get a cue. (See the ball reaction drills on the DVD.)

Youngsters sometimes struggle with agility drills because it takes strength and experience to master agility. That's where a strength program and a conditioning program really come together. As you develop your legs you can plant and have the necessary strength to stop your body and change direction. So don't get frustrated in the early part of your program. Focus on keeping your knees bent, your center of gravity low, your base wide, and changing direction as quickly as possible.

Conditioning for Position-Specific Agility

▲ Lineman and skilled players can benefit from a mix of general and position–specific agility drills.

When high school, college and professional players work on agility drills, the entire team participates. For position-specific agility drills, four or five different drills can be used, such as a drill specific to linemen. Five different drills can be set up, and then every position can rotate through those different drills. By working these drills, even though you may not necessarily need that particular drill for your position, you would increase your overall agility and there would be some carryover effect to your position.

It's not vitally important for you to get position-specific with your agility work. Some specificity is good, but general agility drills are also good because in your teens you're still learning how to handle your own body weight, how to move in space, and how to react to what's going on around you. The point is that there are position-specific fundamental footwork drills that each position should do. They should be limited to one or two in any training session. The rest of the session would be general movement type agilities such as the cone drill for linemen, or the pass-rush drill where the defensive linemen have to move on the snap of the ball and reach the quarterback seven yards back in the pocket.

Skilled and Non-Skilled Groups

For the sake of simplicity it may be best to divide players into two groups: "linemen" (non-skilled) and "skill positions." "Lineman" refers to all offensive and defensive lineman. "Skill players" are everybody else. The basic difference is that linemen are going to do a shorter distance for sprint work because in the course of an actual game, they don't sprint very far. The skill guys—linebackers, wide receivers, running backs, defensive backs, and quarterbacks—generally have to run more during a game, so in conditioning they do more sprint work at longer distances. Whereas linemen only need to practice and prepare for events that unfold within about five yards of them, skill players frequently find themselves twenty, thirty or even eighty yards downfield.

Using a lot of drills involving change of direction is recommended. One of them which is featured on the DVD is the *starburst* drill. To do the star-

The Starburst Drill

burst, arrange five cones in a square with one in the center. Start at one corner of the square and, keeping a low center of gravity, dash to the center and out to another corner cone, then back to the center and out to the next corner cone. This is a great example of the kind of position-specific agility work done in the NFL.

Offense vs. Defense

It's recommended that offensive and defensive linemen work together and build an aerobic base early. Close to the season, a coach can divide them up and have them do drills that relate more directly to their positions. Since offensive linemen need to fire off the ball, stay low, keep their feet moving, and pull along the line of scrimmage, coaches can have players use cones for footwork drills and have them hit blocking dummies. Defensive linemen have to learn to react to the movement of the football, so they will practice coming off the football. Essentially, the offensive guys work by sound and the defensive players work by sight.

For an offensive linemen, a coach can start him in a three-point stance and place a small, red cone (the imaginary opponent) directly in front of him. The coach would give the offensive lineman a snap count, and on the count he's got to burst out of his stance and straddle that cone as he practices his technique. That's his landmark—that's what he's blocking: Then move the cone so that instead of being right in front of him it's now in front of his right foot. He has to get over the cone by stepping more towards the outside edge and getting his body in position. Move the cone from head-up, to right, to left. Each time he's got to take the proper steps coming off the football, keeping his back flat and blocking the cone as though it's a man.

> **It's recommended that offensive and defensive linemen work together and build an aerobic base early. Close to the season, a coach can divide them up . . .**

A coach can work an offensive lineman by adjusting the cone and having him come off on a cadence to block an imaginary defender. A defensive lineman would be rushing the passer. The coach would put the cone where the imaginary offensive lineman is, whether it's a guard or a tackle. Line that marker up across from him, and he would go when the ball moves—accelerating off the line. If some blocking dummies were available the coach could set up one so the defensive lineman could make a pass-rush move on it. Then the player would rush to a point five to seven yards behind the line of scrimmage where there would be another cone or another dummy—simulating a rush on the passer.

Of course, offensive linemen have to strike their opponents. So they need to do drills to prepare their wrists, elbows, and hands for doing that.

> *. . . offensive linemen have to strike their opponents. So they need to do drills to prepare their wrists, elbows, and hands . . .*

One drill to use: Hang a heavy bag and get an offensive lineman to line up in front of it. He holds his stance until the snap count, and then he'll come out of his stance. Now he can strike the bag with his hands and run through the defender.

Defensive players can also utilize heavy bags. They can use them to practice their own pass rush moves. These bags help prepare or condition hands, wrists, elbows, and shoulders for hitting. Start off working these drills easy and as you get in better condition over time, strike harder and harder. That way, once you get into a football situation you can get physical and not risk injury.

Linebackers need to work on visual cues. One way to do this: Linebackers line up off the line of scrimmage at a distance they would be in a game. Then they are given a visual cue—run or pass. If it's a run they've got designated areas that they have to sprint to, so if it's a sweep left he's got a place to be. He's got a pursuit angle that he needs to take to intersect that runner and he needs to be sprinting towards the line of scrimmage to hit that spot. If there's a blocking dummy that he could hit when he gets there, that's even better.

Another visual cue would be a pass. The linebacker would have to turn and drop to a designated area. If you have someone available, throw a football into that area so he can get used to dropping into coverage, seeing a football coming into that area, and intercepting it.

For a defensive back, it would be a similar situation. He would line up off the football in his designated area. He would have to read run or pass. In the case of a run he would have to come up to an area that would be his position to contain if it was coming his way. If the run is to the other side, he's got to turn and get in the pursuit lane to intersect the play going away from him. If he gets a pass cue, then he has to drop in his zone just like the linebacker and be ready to defend a particular area against the pass.

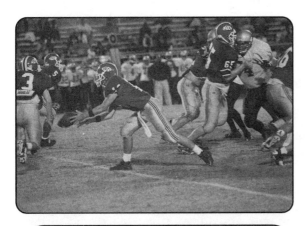

▲ It's vitally important for quarterbacks to work on their fundamental footwork.

Footwork

As a result, defensive backs and linebackers need to work on *backpedaling*. Backpedaling is used to get into pass coverage, but it also makes for an excellent warm-up. There are two styles of backpedaling: There's the classic style in which you move from the ball of one foot and push off onto the ball of the other foot. There is also a newer method that a lot of coaches are teaching today. With this method you move your weight off the ball of one foot and roll it onto your heel. Then the other foot comes down, and the weight goes onto the ball of that foot. As you're going backwards, bring your heel up to you rear end and reach back and let the ball roll to the heel as you're coming upwards with the other foot. Either technique works, it's just a matter of preference. It's not unlike planting the foot to move forward after a series of backpedals—some coaches teach their players to plant their lead foot slightly sideways so they get more cleats in the ground and better traction.

It's vitally important for quarterbacks to work on their fundamental footwork. Whether a guy is opening up to hand the ball to an off-tackle runner or whether he's pitching a ball to a tailback running around the end, he needs to practice these fundamentals every single day. He needs to work on his footwork from the standpoint of taking a drop. Whether it's a three-, five- or seven-step drop, he needs to be a certain distance from the line of scrimmage before he passes because the linemen who protect him are counting on his being in that spot. Even footwork on the actual pass is critical. Another NFLCA book, *How to Grow a Winning Quarterback,* by long-time NFL quarterback coach Jerry Rhome, features DVD instruction by Peyton Manning and Drew Bledsoe. It's an excellent resource for quarterback-specific training and tips.

Agility Drills by Position

The following is a rundown of agility exercises by position. During the months of June and July your running workouts should include the activities listed for your position. For example, receivers should be running routes; defensive backs should be backpedaling; offensive and defensive linemen should be working on takeoff, change of direction, etc.
Perform the following drills along with any other agility, speed, and sprint work you need. Start with:

■ Warm-up run: 600 to 800 yards.
■ Flexibility and stretching: 15 minutes.
■ Six starts at 10 to 15 yards each.

After completing the above, execute the agility drills for your position as instructed on the pages that follow.

Defensive Backs

- Stance backpedal at half-speed for 15 yards; repeat twice.
- Stance backpedal at three-quarter speed for 15 yards; repeat twice.
- Stance backpedal at full speed for 15 yards; repeat four times.
- Lateral shuffle: 15 yards right, 15 yards left, backpedal 5 yards, then turn and sprint 10 yards.
- Stance backpedal: 90 degree sprint 15 yards; repeat five times to the right, five to the left.
- Stance backpedal: 15 yards, turn 135 degrees, sprint burst 15 yards; repeat five times right and five times left.
- Stance backpedal: 15 yards, 180 degree sprint 15 yards; repeat five times.
- Stance backpedal: down a line, swivel right, swivel left, right and left, six times each way for 30 yards.
- Stance backpedal: shuffle 10 yards, sprint and break forward 10 yards; complete eight times.
- Stance backpedal: turn and run 15 yards and burst 10 yards.

Linebackers

- Sprint starts from stance: 15 yards, repeat 10 times.
- Stance pass: drop seven to 12 yards, turn 45 degrees, left, right; do ten times each.
- High-knee lateral: run 15 yards, 8 times–four right and four left.
- Shuttle runs: Sprint 5 yards, sprint back to start. Sprint 10 yards, sprint back to start; repeat eight times.
- Lateral shuttle runs: 5 yards to the left, pivot and run 10 yards to your right, pivot, turn and run 5 yards back to the start.
- Pass-drop: backpedal 10 yards, break and sprint forward 10 yards; repeat five times at 45 degrees right and 45 degrees left.
- Run in place for 5 seconds, belly slam on turf, get up, seat roll right, seat roll left, get up and sprint 10 yards; repeat eight times.
- Lay five dummies or towels in a straight line about two yards apart. Slalom through and sprint 10 yards.

Linemen (Offensive and Defensive)

- Sprint starts from stance: 15 yards, repeat 10 times.
- High-knee run: 15 yards, repeat 6 times.
- Karioka: 15 yards, repeat 6 times.
- Run in place five seconds, seat roll right, seat roll left, get up and sprint 10 yards; repeat six times.
- Stance, stay square, shuffle Mirror drill, ten to the left and ten to the right.
- Foot movement work. Jump rope or sprint (use either one), 10 sets of 10 seconds each with 30 seconds rest. Finish with non-stop jump for 1 minute then rest, jump rope for 2 minutes then rest and jump rope for 5 minutes then rest.

Agility Drill Stance

- Stance sprint 10 yards, turn 90 degrees, sprint 10 yards, five to the left and five to the right.
- Shuttle runs: Start line sprint 5 yards, sprint back to the start, sprint 10 yards and sprint back to the start; repeat ten times.

Running Backs

- Sprint starts from stance: 15 yards, repeat 6 times.
- Stance sprint: 15 yards 90 degrees cut, ten times right and ten times left.
- Stance motion right/left 10 yards, turn sprint 15 yards, ten times left and ten times right.
- Stance: start sprint 15 yards, cut back 5 yards.
- Stance: start sprint 15 yards, cut 2 steps right, 2 steps left, burst 10 yards, accelerate 10 more yards.

■ Stance start: 20-yard sprint, stride 20 yards, sprint 20 yards, 60 yards total; repeat ten times.

■ Shuttle runs: 40 yards, sprint 10 yards, cut and sprint back to the start, sprint back to the 10, sprint back to the start (40 yards total). Repeat 8 times.

■ Karioka: 20 yards, repeat 8 times.

Quarterbacks

■ Stance: 3-step, 5-step and 7-step drops, ten to fifteen times each.

■ Three-step, 5-step and 7-step drop. Wait four seconds. Sprint out 45 degrees to the right and to the left, 10 yards each, ten times each. Repeat 10 times.

■ Stance sprint out and/or option steps right and left, fifteen times at 10 to 12 yards each.

■ Work out throwing all pass routes.

■ Shuffle runs same as No.7 listing for running backs.

Receivers and Tight Ends

■ Stance start: 15 yards single hand catches, ten each hand.

■ Stance start: 15 yard sprint, burst 10 yards, catch.

■ Stance start: 10 yard spring, cut 45 degrees right, 2 steps cut 45 degrees left, 2 steps burst 10 yards sprints.

■ Stance start: 15 yard sprint, 90 degree cut, sprint 15 yards. Do ten to the right and ten to the left.

■ Work on sprint takeoff, bursts, breaks and cuts at top speed. 15 to 20 yards with 2 or 3 moves on each route.

■ Work on catching over both shoulders.

■ Shuttle runs: 60 yards. Start sprint to 5 yard line. Cut back to the start, cut sprint to the 10 yard line. Back to the start, sprint to the 15 yard line, cut and sprint back to the start. Repeat 6 times.

Track 14

Agility Games

These drills can help any player improve agility.

Starburst Drill

Set up five cones or other markers as shown in the DVD. Have a coach, friend, or teammate stand in front of the forward middle cone. He will point in random order to all five cones, and you must hustle and touch each designated cone and return to your starting point.

CHANGE OF DIRECTION DRILLS

◀ Z-X Drill

Start facing the coach. Shuffle ten yards to start, the run up fifteen yards in a diagonal pattern. Once again, shuffle ten yards, make the turn and run fifteen yards in a diagonal pattern.

Tag Drill ▶

Start with one player in front of another facing front to back. The back player should have one hand on the hip of the front player. The player in front should begin to run forward and then change direction, speed up, and slow down. The object is for the front player to either shake the back player or force the back player to run into him.

Mirror Drill

Have two players position themselves five
yards apart, facing each other. One player will
lead the drill. As the leading player moves
forward, the other should move backwards
just as the reflection in a mirror would do.
If the leader shuffles left and raises his right
hand, the follower needs to shuffle right and
raise his left hand.

Pattern Running

Once you have developed a conditioning base,
you can begin a heightened phase of your
agility work. Pattern running is a position-
specific exercise that mimics the running patterns a player will make in a game.

On pp. 64-72, you will see spider-like pattern running charts for each
position. Above each chart is a key that explains the pattern abbreviations.
For instance, at the top of the defensive line chart there is a straight line
with "20S" beside it. The key above the chart explains that this is a twenty-
yard sprint. By using the diagram and the key, you will know exactly what
form each pattern will take.

Below each chart is a box detailing six repetitions for each position. For
instance, for defensive linemen, the first rep begins with a ten-yard sprint.
That's followed by a S5P15L, which means sprint five yards, turn and pur-
sue fifteen yards left. After the first series of ten patterns, *take a three-
minute rest* and move on to the second rep. Then take three minutes rest
after each rep.

Early on, only try one or two reps. As your conditioning improves, add
one level. Even well-conditioned NFL players find this routine difficult, so
build slowly.

Pattern Running
Defensive Line

20S	20 yard Sprint	
S5P15R	Sprint 5 Pursuit 15 Right	
S5P15L	Sprint 5 Pursuit 15 Left	
CR10P10R	Crossover Run 10 Pursuit 10 Right	
CR10P10L	Crossover Run 10 Pursuit 10 Left	
CR10A5R	Crossover Run 10 Attack 5 Right	
CR10A5L	Crossover Run 10 Attack 5 Left	
SH5P10R	Shuffle 5 Pursuit 10 Right	

SH5P10L	Shuffle 5 Pursuit 10 Left
SH5A5R	Shuffle 5 Attack 5 Right
SH5A5L	Shuffle 5 Attack 5 Left
10S	10 yard Sprint
5S	5 yard Sprint
5SLR	5 yard Slant Right
5SLL	5 yard Slant Left

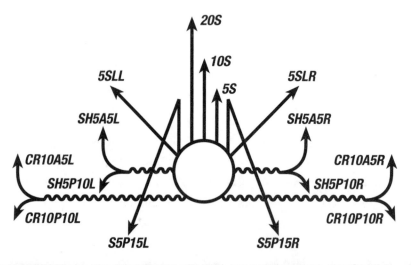

	1	2	3	4	5	6
1	10S	20S	CR10A5R	CR10P10R	S5P15R	SH5P10R
2	S5P15L	CR10A5L	SH5A5L	5SLR	CR10P10R	SH5A5L
3	SH5A5R	S5P15R	5S	SH5P10L	20S	5SLR
4	SHSA5L	SH5P10R	SH5A5R	SH5A5L	CR10A5L	SH5P10L
5	5SLL	CR10P10R	CR10A5L	20S	10S	CR10A5L
6	S5P15R	CR10A5R	SH5P10L	CR10P10L	20S	10S
7	5SLR	SH5P10L	5SLL	5SLL	CR10P10L	5S
8	CR10P10L	S5P15L	SH5P10R	SH5P10R	S5P15L	5S
9	CR10P10R	CR10P10L	5SLR	5S	CR10A5R	SH5A5L
10	20S	5S	10S	SH5A5R	20S	5SLL

Chart shows six repetitions of ten patterns

Pattern Running
Inside Linebackers

30S	30 yard Sprint	
20S	20 yard Sprint	
15DDR	15 yard Drop and Drive Right	
15DDL	15 yard Drop and Drive Left	
15DPR	15 yard Drop Right	
15DPL	15 yard Drop Left	
15BP	15 yard Backpedal	
10S	10 yard Sprint	

10CRR	10 yard Crossover Run Right
10CRL	10 yard Crossover Run Left
5S	5 yard Sprint
5DR	5 yard Drive Right
5DL	5 yard Drive Left
5AR	5 yard Attack Right
5AL	5 yard Attack Left

	1	2	3	4	5	6
1	5DR	30S	5DL	20S	30S	15DDR
2	15DDL	10CRR	15DDR	15BP	15DDR	5AL
3	15BP	5S	15DDL	5S	10CRL	15DPL
4	5AL	30S	5DR	5DR	30S	5DR
5	20S	10CRL	15BP	10S	15DPL	15DDL
6	5DL	15DPL	10CRL	5AR	10 CRR	15DPR
7	5AR	15DPR	10S	10CRL	20S	5S
8	15DDR	20S	10CRR	5AL	15DDL	5AR
9	5S	5AL	15DPR	10CRR	10DPR	5DL
10	10S	5AR	15DPL	5DL	15BP	10S

Chart shows six repetitions of ten patterns

Pattern Running
Outside Linebackers

30SWR	30 yard Swing Right	**150PSHSPR**	15 yard Option Shuffle Sprint Right
30SWL	30 yard Swing Left	**150PSHSPL**	15 yard Option Shuffle Sprint Left
30SER	30 yard Seam Right	**10FLATR**	10 yard Flat Attack Right
30SEL	30 yard Seam Left	**10FLATL**	10 yard Flat Attack Left
20FLATR	20 yard Flat Right	**10PRR**	10 yard Pass Rush Right
20FLATL	20 yard Flat Left	**10PRL**	10 yard Pass Rush Left
15HL	15 yard Hook Right	**10DL**	10 yard Draw Right
15HL	15 yard Hook Left	**10DL**	10 yard Draw Left

	1	2	3	4	5	6
1	15HL	10DR	30SER	10PRL	15HL	15HR
2	10FLATL	20FLR	10DL	30SWL	30SER	10DL
3	30SWR	30SWR	15HR	150PHSPR	10 FLATL	30SER
4	150PSHSPR	10PRL	10FLATR	10DL	20FLR	10PRL
5	20FLL	3CSER	150SHSR	20FLR	30SWL	150PSHSPR
6	15HR	10DL	10FLATL	10PRR	10FLATR	10DR
7	20FLR	30SEL	150SHSL	150PSHSPL	30SEL	150PSHSPL
8	10FLATR	20FLR	15HL	20FLL	30SWR	15HL
9	150PSHSPL	10PRR	10DR	10DR	15HR	10PRR
10	30SWL	30SWL	30SEL	30SWR	20FLL	30SEL

Chart shows six repetitions of ten patterns

Pattern Running
Defensive Backs

30S	30 yard Sprint
20S	20 yard Sprint
20BPPRS	20 yard Backpedal Pivot Right Sprint
20BPPLS	20 yard Backpedal Pivot Left Sprint
15BP	15 yard Backpedal
10S	10 yard Sprint
10DR	10 yard Drive Right
10DL	10 yard Drive Left
10BPDR	10 yard Backpedal Drive Right
10BPDL	10 yard Backpedal Drive Left
OHR7BR	Open Hips Run 7 Break Right
OHR7BL	Open Hips Run 7 Break Left
5BPDR	5 yard BackPedal Drive Right
5BPDL	5 yard BackPedal Drive Left
5SHR	5 yard Shuffle Right
5SHL	5 yard Shuffle Left

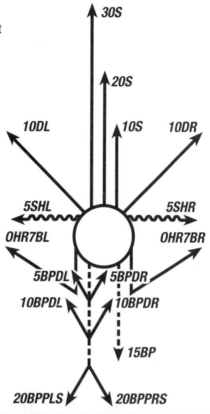

	1	2	3	4	5	6
1	5SHR	20BPPLS	5SHL	20S	30S	5BPDR
2	10DR	30S	10DL	15BP	15BP	5SHL
3	OHR7BL	5BPDR	OHR7BR	OHR7BL	10DL	OHR7BR
4	10BPDR	20BPPRS	10BPDL	10S	30S	5BPDL
5	5SHL	20S	5SHR	5BPDL	10DR	5SHR
6	15BP	5BPDL	OHR7BL	20BPPRS	20BPPRS	10S
7	30S	20BPPRS	5BPDL	OHR7BR	10BPDL	10DL
8	OHR7BR	15BP	10DL	20BPPLS	20S	OHR7BL
9	10DL	20BPPLS	5BPDR	10S	10BPDR	10DR
10	10BPDL	10S	10BPDR	5BPDR	20BPPLS	20S

Chart shows six repetitions of ten patterns

67

Pattern Running
Offensive Line

20S	20 yard Sprint	**5RR**	5 yard Reach Right
15S	15 yard Sprint	**5RL**	5 yard Reach Left
15PPR	15 yard Pass Pro Right	**5AR**	5 yard Angle Right
15PPL	15 yard Pass Pro Left	**5AL**	5 yard Angle Left
10S	10 yard Sprint	**5DLR**	5 yard Down the Line Right
10PDR	10 yard Pull and Hip Right	**5DLL**	5 yard Down the Line Left
10PDL	10 yard Pull and Hip Left	**5PPFR**	5 yard Pass Pro Flat Right
5D	5 yard Drive	**5PPFL**	5 yard Pass Pro Flat Left

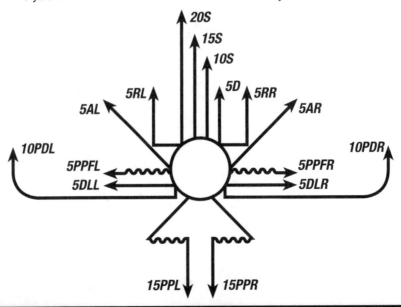

	1	2	3	4	5	6
1	10PDL	20S	15PPL	10S	20S	5AR
2	15PPR	5D	5AR	5PPFL	10PDR	10S
3	5PPFR	10PDL	15S	20S	15PPL	5PPFL
4	10PDR	15PPL	5PPFL	5DLL	5DLR	10PDL
5	5AR	5RR	5DLR	5D	15S	5D
6	5RL	15S	20S	15S	10PDL	5PPFR
7	15PPL	5RL	5AL	5DLR	15PPR	5RL
8	5PPFL	10PDR	5PPFR	5PPFR	10S	10PDR
9	5AL	15PPR	5DLL	5RR	5DLL	5RR
10	5RR	10S	15PPR	5RL	20S	5AL

Chart shows six repetitions of ten patterns

Pattern Running
Tight Ends

30STR	30 yard Streak Right
30STL	30 yard Streak Left
30LPAC	30 yard Lean, Plant, Accelerate
25TOR	25 yard Take-off Right
25TOL	25 yard Take-off Left
15CCR	15 yard Cross-Country Right
15CCL	15 yard Cross-Country Left
15SHUPR	15 yard Shuffle Up Right

15SHUPL	15 yard Shuffle Up Left
10HR	10 yard Hook Right
10HL	10 yard Hook Left
5FR	5 yard Flat Right
5FL	5 yard Flat Left
5SS	5 yard Stance-Start
5PSPR	5 yard Pass Set Power Right
5PSPL	5 yard Pass Set Power Left

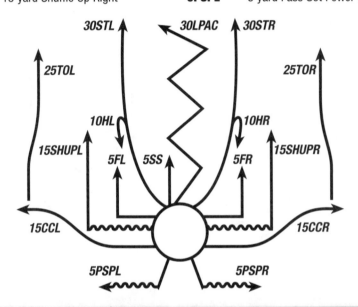

	1	2	3	4	5	6
1	5SS	30STR	25TOR	30LPAC	15SHUPL	5SS
2	15CCR	10HL	15SHUPR	5SS	5FLR	15SHUPR
3	15SHUPR	5FLR	30STL	30STL	30STL	30LPAC
4	5PSPL	25TOL	5FLL	10HR	5PSPR	5PSPR
5	30LPAC	5PSPL	5SS	25TOR	15CCR	15CCL
6	10HL	10HR	5FLR	15SHUPR	5PSPL	25TOL
7	15CCL	5FLL	30STR	15SHUPL	30STR	15CCR
8	10HR	25TOL	25TOL	25TOL	5SFL	5PSPL
9	15SHUPL	5PSPL	15SHUPL	10HL	15CCL	25TOR
10	5PSPR	30STL	30LPAC	30STR	15SHUPR	15SHUPL

Chart shows six repetitions of ten patterns

Pattern Running
Runningbacks/Fullbacks

30WHR	30 yard Wheel Right	**15SWR**	15 yard Swing Right
30WHL	30 yard Wheel Left	**15SWL**	15 yard Swing Left
30ST	30 yard Streak	**15ARR**	15 yard Arrow Right
25POR	25 yard Pogo Right	**15ARL**	15 yard Arrow Left
25POL	25 yard Pogo Left	**15DLR**	15 yard Delay Right
20CHR	20 yard Choice Right	**15DLL**	15 yard Delay Left
20CHL	20 yard Choice Left	**10DR**	10 yard Drive Right
15LBC	15 Linebacker Control	**10DL**	10 yard Drive Left

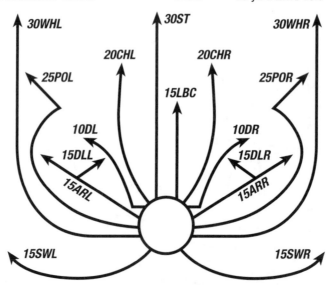

	1	2	3	4	5	6
1	10DR	30WHR	20CHL	30ST	30WHL	15SWR
2	15LBC	15ARL	10DR	15SWR	30ST	20CHL
3	15DLL	25POR	15ARL	10DL	30WHL	15SWL
4	20CHR	15LBC	25POR	15LBC	25POR	15DLR
5	15SWL	15SWR	20CHR	15SWL	30WL	25POL
6	10DL	25POL	25POL	15DLR	20CHR	15ARL
7	15DLR	30WHL	15DLL	15ARL	25POL	25POR
8	20CHL	15SWL	15ARR	15DEL	30WHR	15ARR
9	30ST	15ARR	15DLL	10DR	20CHL	20CHR
10	15SWR	30ST	15DLR	15ARL	15LBC	15DLL

Chart shows six repetitions of ten patterns

Pattern Running
Receivers

9	40 yards
TAKE-OFF	30 yards
DRAG	30 yards
8	25 yards
7	20 yards
6	15 yards
5	15 yards
4	15 yards
3	10 yards
2	5 yards
1	5 yards
0	5 yards
5SHR	5 yard Shuffle Right
5SHL	5 yard Shuffle Left
5SS	5 yard Stance and Start

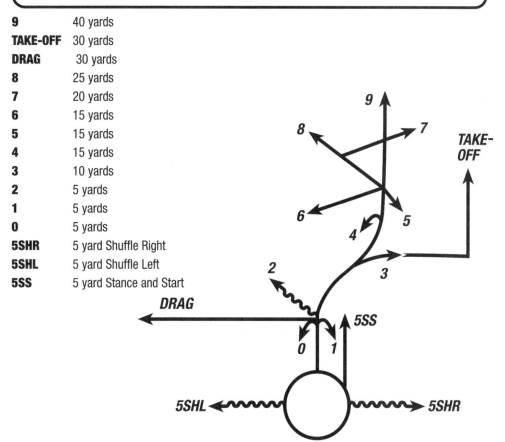

	1	2	3	4	5	6
1	0	5SHL	9	0	4	5SHR
2	5	8	7	1	5SHL	5SHL
3	5SHR	4	5	4	0	5SS
4	TAKE-OFF	3	8	3	5SHR	9
5	DRAG	1	6	TAKE-OFF	2	9
6	5SS	9	5SS	DRAG	1	TAKE-OFF
7	9	5SS	5SHR	7	3	5
8	6	2	5SHL	8	9	8
9	2	5SHR	TAKE-OFF	5	6	7
10	7	6	DRAG	5SS	DRAG	4

Chart shows six repetitions of ten patterns

Pattern Running
Quarterbacks

30S	30 yard Sprint	**15SOL**	15 yard Sprint-out Left
25S	25 yard Sprint	**10S**	10 yard Sprint
20S	20 yard Sprint	**10ROR**	10 yard Roll-out Right
15S	15 yard Sprint	**10ROL**	10 yard Roll-out Left
15OR	15 yard Option Right	**7SDR**	7 Step Drop
15OL	15 yard Option Left	**5SDR**	5 Step Drop
15SOR	15 yard Sprint-out Right	**3SDR**	3 yard Drop

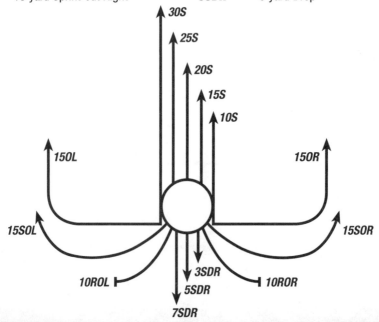

	1	2	3	4	5	6
1	15S	30S	7SDR	15SOR	30S	10ROR
2	15OR	25S	25S	15SOL	15OR	10S
3	3SDR	20S	3SDR	7SDR	15SOL	15SOL
4	7SDR	10S	15OR	7SDR	30S	10ROL
5	15OL	15SOR	5SDR	5SDR	15OL	15SOR
6	30S	7SDR	15OL	30S	15SOR	7SDR
7	10ROR	5SDR	20S	10S	25S	5SDR
8	10ROL	3SDR	10ROR	15OR	20S	3SDR
9	5SDR	15SOL	10ROL	15OL	15S	20S
10	10S	30S	15S	25S	3SDR	15S

Chart shows six repetitions of ten patterns

ChapterSix
Types of Conditioning

Aerobic vs. Anaerobic Conditioning

There are two basic types of conditioning work, aerobic and anaerobic. Each employs a different body system. *Aerobic*, which means "with oxygen," usually describes longer duration, lower stress exercises such as walking. Depending on how far you go, walking simply relies on your oxygen intake for fuel; therefore it's an aerobic exercise.

Anaerobic means "without oxygen." It's usually a more aggressive exercise of shorter duration, such as a sprint or the lifting of a weight. These bursts of activity do not call on the aerobic system for fuel. In fact, you can do many anaerobic exercises without even breathing. Instead, anaerobic exercises utilize the anaerobic system. That is, they burn up less oxygen and rely more on the body's glycogen stores.

▲ Weightlifting, with its quick bursts of energy, is an example of an anaerobic exercise.

▲ A sprint is an anaerobic exercise because although it involves running, there's a quick burst of energy that doesn't require prolonged heavy breathing.

Depending on the duration of the exercise, an aerobic activity could become an anaerobic activity. Imagine a sprint that turned into a marathon. Aerobic exercise means an exercise such as long-distance running that requires heavy breathing. An anaerobic exercise is usually a shorter exercise such as a sprint or a two-to five-second drill simulating a football play.

The reason you need a minimum of six weeks in a conditioning program is that it gives you one or two weeks to prepare your body with a little bit of an aerobic base. You would still add some anaerobic drills to start preparing for it, and then you could take four weeks and really hone in on developing yourself for football practice.

Let's break down a basic aerobic conditioning program. The aerobic part of the program will consist of runs and activities that are longer than you can hold your breath. For instance, if you are doing a jog or a stride—running at a speed at which you can still carry on a casual conversation—then you are working at an aerobic level. Once you pick up the pace to a point where you can't talk or you can't really breathe without heavy breathing then you are in anaerobic phase. So as you get started, you just want to run at a level that will allow you to get your body adjusted to a physical conditioning program.

Treadmills have become very popular for aerobic exercise, but try not to use a treadmill for football training. It's better to run outside on grass. Treadmills do too much of the work, plus the act of running on a treadmill is nothing like the act of running on turf. You want to condition yourself in a manner as close as possible to the activity that you are going to be performing on the field. Football players do not play football on treadmills; they play it on grass. So you should run on a grass or Astroturf® field. If that's not feasible, the next best option is a tartan track that has some give to it. Training on asphalt or concrete would be a last resort. These last two surfaces are a little too hard. They don't give when you plant your foot. In fact, if you are training on a real hard surface over a period of time you are actually going to *create* injury situations rather than prevent them as conditioning is intended to do.

If you are on a natural grass field, you need to have cleats on. You don't want to be running around in tennis shoes because you are likely to slip on the grass and injure yourself. A pulled groin or a strained hamstring is the last thing you need when you're in a conditioning program. If you are working out on an Astroturf field or any of the other surfaces you can get by with a good fitting tennis or running shoe.

Plyometric Conditioning

Consider two kinds of vertical jumps. In the first one, you squat down into a quarter or half-squat position, hold that for three or four seconds, and then jump. In the second, you start with your
knees just slightly bent and in one motion dip down and jump up as fast as you can. Which one will allow you to jump higher? The second one will. Why? Because the first technique—the one with the pause—requires you to overcome your own inertia before you can bring your body up. In the second method, the quick dip-and-jump, you create energy by stretching those muscles real fast and then contracting them real fast. If you stretch those muscles and stop for a moment, that energy is reduced.

That's a lesson in an area of conditioning called *plyometrics*. Plyometrics are specialized training drills that are done in sets and repetitions just like weight training exercises. The word "plyometric" comes from the Greek word *pleythyein*, which means "to increase." These power development drills first gained recognition at the Munich Olympics (1972) after Soviet sprinter Valery Borzov trained with them and became the Olympic champion in both the 100- and 200-meter events. Since that time, plyometrics have been an integral part of nearly all high-level speed and power training programs.

Plyometrics employ that stretch/reflex mechanism discussed above. They make use of the energy that's created in the rapid stretching and contracting of muscles. The more rapid the contraction the more powerful the result. Plyometrics are a terrific way to build power because they speed up the contraction. They can really contribute to your explosiveness. They bridge the gap between the relatively slow strength training of the weight room and the explosive speed required on the playing field. Through a carefully applied plyometric program, you can teach your nervous system to recruit more muscle fibers at a greater rate in order to create more force at a given joint angle. In other words, you become a stronger, more powerful athlete.

> *. . . plyometrics have been an integral part of nearly all high-level speed and power training programs.*

The Scientific Rules of Plyometrics:

- Maximum tension develops when active muscle is stretched quickly.
- The faster a muscle is forced to lengthen, the greater the tension it exerts.
- The rate of the stretch is more important than the magnitude of the stretch.

When you do a plyometric exercise, such as the jump described above, you don't want to stay on the ground very long. In fact, when it comes to plyometrics, it's less important how high you jump than how quickly you get off the ground. A quick jump means your muscles are contracting quickly. A poorly conditioned player will be so saddled by the downward inertia of his own body weight that it will appear as though he is sinking into the floor even when he is trying to jump.

Plyometrics have been around a long time, and they appear in everyday activities. For instance, when you run you are jumping from one leg to another in a plyometric fashion. There are plenty of ways to incorporate plyometrics into your conditioning. Some coaches toss a medicine ball towards a player and have the player punch it. If you are in a push-up position and you do a push-up, a hand clap, and then go back to the push-up position, that's plyometrics. Or if you are in a push-up position with blocks near your hands and you push your body up and land with your hands on top of the blocks, that would be plyometrics.

People tend to get caught up in plyometrics, and they can take on pretty strenuous exercises. Whether it's weights or plyometrics, it's better to start small and gradually increase the challenge rather that to start too big and risk failure or even injury.

Plyometric Exercises

You can apply plyometrics to the legs by doing simple jumping exercises. For instance, in *box jumps* (which are demonstrated in detail on the DVD), you will jump off and onto a pedestal or a block, keeping your time on the ground to an absolute minimum. The block does not have to be very high, even a few inches will do. But the key is the turnaround time—how long it takes you to go from heading down to heading up. The shorter that turnaround, the more powerful and explosive a football player you'll be. What you're really trying to tell your brain is that you want to react to the ground very quickly. It's almost as though the ground is a hot plate and you're barefooted. So as soon as you hit it, you want to be able to react and jump from that. When doing these types of drills, you are learning to handle your body weight in a very quick movement, and that's going to directly relate to agility drills when you're starting to change direction. See p.90 for more information on box jumps.

How do plyometrics mesh with strength training, particularly free weights? One supports the other. Free weights develop strength in the muscles that will allow you to do a plyometric exercise. Now, if you are doing a *hand clean*, that in itself could be considered a plyometric exercise because you're getting a stretch from the quadriceps in order to lift that weight. When you do a *squat* exercise, that's really developing the strength in your legs. So when you do a jumping drill and you land, you've got enough leg strength to stop your downward movement and change that into an upward movement. *Note: The basic rules and guidelines of plyometrics are simple but very important. Since plyometrics are high-intensity, all-out drills, it's important to keep the following in mind:*

- Do NOT do plyometric drills more than twice a week.
- Always do plyometric drills on forgiving surfaces.
- Emphasize quality over quantity. More is not always better.
- ALWAYS warm up and stretch prior to doing plyometrics.
- Do plyometric drills when fresh, prior to weight training and running.
- Use laced footwear that offers support for the ankles and the arches.

Here are some of the plyometric exercises that are included on our six-week conditioning program. Remember that the key to these plyometric exercises is spending as little time on the ground as possible. (See the DVD for demonstrations of these exercises.)

The Basic Plyometric Position

Most plyometric jumps begin in an upright stance similar to that used by a tailback. That is:

- Chest over knees over toes.

- Body weight centered in the front half of each foot.
- Arms flexed at the elbow, approximately ninety degrees.
- Shoulders hyper-extended so that the upper arms are nearly parallel to the ground.
- Ankle "locked," affording little or no dorsiflexion on takeoff or landing.

The basic move for most plyometric jumps is to drive both arms simultaneously upwards and quickly "block" (or suddenly stop) the arm drive when your hands reach about eye level. This transfers the power generated in the arm swing to the body. At the same time as you block your arm movement, explode off the ground with a maximal or near-maximal jump. While in the air, re-cock your shoulders and legs so you land in the starting plyometric position, ready to explode into the air immediately upon contact with the ground. The less time your feet spend on the ground, the better.

Try to avoid:

- Excessive trunk flexion-extension as this can cause an overload on the lower back.
- Over-reaching and landing on your heels as this will dampen the stretch reflex.
- Staggered-step landings or takeoffs. These can place undue stress on one leg.

Try to maximize:

- Loose relaxed hands.
- Heel lift toward the buttocks and knee-toe drive up in front.
- A mental concept of quick, light, and explosive movement off the ground.
- Arm drive to eye level with effective "blocking."
- Upright, tight body position in order to handle the load on the hips and minimize back stress.

Most of the following plyometric drills are demonstrated on the DVD. It is strongly suggested that you view it before attempting them.

◀ *Power Skip*

Begin to skip in a sprinter's skip action, utilizing great technique (elbow at ninety degrees; knee-toe up; good triple extension on the support leg; straight back; head held high; eye focus downrange). After two or three skips, begin to explode into the air, concentrating on great drive with the lift leg and arms. When in mid-air, freeze in the skip position for a split second before you begin to uncoil for the next repetition. *Do not* over-reach with your lead foot, hitting the ground with your heel first. Instead, you must drive the lead foot straight down under the knee in order to properly contact the ground with the front half of the foot.

◀ *Power Shuffle*

This power drill is executed as any standard shuffle drill. You will move laterally and lead step as you simultaneously push off the far support leg. Your lead step foot should make contact with the ground first, followed closely by your trailing push-off foot. Your stance at this time should still be about shoulder-width, with your weight on the inside part of the balls of your feet. Each step should be powerful and explosive in nature. The arms should be used for maximum power with little regard to technique.

◀ *Power Karioka*

This is the old karioka drill, executed by lead stepping, crossover stepping (in front), lead stepping, and crossover stepping (behind). However, as you gain speed you should explode off of each step, forcefully pushing off the support leg while driving the swing leg laterally in a lead step, crossing over or reaching behind with great power. Try to cover as much ground as possible while maintaining your weight balanced on the balls or front half of your foot. Again, the arms should be used for maximum power with little regard to technique.

◀ *Tuck Jump*

Begin in the basic plyometric position. Jump vertically into the air, driving either the heels to the buttocks or the knees-toes to the chest. The arms should both drive up and block simultaneously. As you progress, learn to drive the heels to the buttocks and the knees to the chest in a cycling motion. As you land in a good cocked position, immediately explode back up into the air, spending as little time on the ground as possible.

Long Jump

This drill is very similar to the tuck jump except that you will add a horizontal element to the vertical jump. That is, you will be jumping both up and forward. Again, the hands will drive and block, the heels will brush the buttocks, and the knees-toes will lift up and through. As soon as you contact the ground—in cocked position—explode into the next repetition.

Standing Triple-Jump

From a standing position, cock the swing leg back as you cock the shoulders/arms, and slightly sit down on the support leg. Now you will drive the arms through and block; drive the swing (left) leg up; and jump off the support (right) leg. The right leg should drive the heel past the buttocks and the knees-toes up and through. The arms should re-cock as the support (right) leg prepares to support the body again. The swing (left) leg should re-cock and prepare to explode again. As soon as ground contact is made, repeat the prior movement. Now, while in the air, the support (right) leg will become the swing leg and the swing (left) leg will now become the support leg. Drive off the new support (left) as the right leg drives knee-toe upward towards the chest. Finally, as you reach out, land in a high position on both feet with knees flexed no deeper than about 110 degrees. All of that is one standing triple jump. As you repeat the repetitions, make sure you switch your support and swing legs so that each leg gets equal work and stress.

Box Jump ▼

The box jump is very well depicted on the DVD. Ideally you have a series of boxes or containers (or specially made stools) that are graduated in height from about eight inches all the way up to forty-plus inches. The idea is to assume the normal plyometric position. Then with good arm drive and blocking and good knee-toe lift, jump on top of the box. Land in the center of the box with weight distributed on both legs. Now, step off the box—DO NOT jump off—and do your next repetition. This exercise requires lots of practice and a spotter, but it's an excellent way to develop explosive power in the legs.

Running Bounds ▶

In running bounds you essentially run slowly but with great vertical lift. Start out with a simple jog and begin to bound from leg to leg with great knee-toe lift and heel-to-buttock drive. It should be much like a triple jump except that you are switch-ing the swing and support legs with each step. The arms should use either a double or single arm drive. Do not over-reach and land on your heels, but land on the full forefoot with the foot directly under the center of the body and explode.

Calf Jumps ▶

Place your hands on your hips. Straighten your legs, using little or no knee flex. Do not allow the knees to bend. Begin to jump straight up as high as possible (don't go forward, only up), using only your calf muscles for propulsion. As soon as you hit the ground, explode again with your next repetition.

Ski Jump (Diagonal Jump)

◀ Begin this drill in the normal, upright plyometric position. This technique is virtually identical to the tuck jump, except you jump both forward and sideways so that you create a zig-zag pattern as you move downrange. Maintain your body weight close to an imaginary center line with each jump being only about eighteen to thirty-six inches, but with good downrange displacement. As always, be quick off the ground, utilize good arm drive/block mechanics, and remember to drive your knees-toes up and over as you go side to side down the field. These are diagonal jumps in which you jump anywhere from eighteen to thirty-six inches as though you are skiing down a slope. A good way to do these is to jump diagonally from the outside of one hash mark to the inside of the next one.

High Split Jump

In a standing position, split your feet front to back with about eighteen

High Split Jump

◀ inches between toe and heel. Put your hands on your hips and keep them there. Sit slightly down, keeping your body weight centered and distributed equally between the front and back feet. Jump vertically into the air and switch the feet, putting the front foot in back and the back foot in front. As you do so, the heels should cycle through and contact the buttocks in a sprinting/cycling fashion. Upon ground contact, explode immediately into the air.

Deep Split Jump

This drill is a variation on the high split jump. In this drill you start with a much bigger split by assuming a lunge position. Cock the arms back as in the normal plyometric technique. As you jump, drive the arms up, blocking them at face height. As you explode vertically, the feet again should switch positions with the heels cycling through the buttocks area.

High Scissor Jumps

◀ In a high split position, with the hands on the hips, jump vertically and switch the feet just like a split jump. However, in this jump there is no cycling motion. The legs should stay fairly straight like scissor blades in order to stress the hip musculature. The speed of the switch is the key to this drill. Be quick off the ground and utilize speed and power in your switch.

Low Scissor Jumps

Begin in a deep lunge position with the arms cocked back in the basic plyometric position. Jump vertically and switch the feet, keeping the legs fairly straight while simultaneously driving and blocking at face level with the arms. As soon as you contact the ground, explode into your next repetition with power and quickness. If you master this simple drill, the next step is to do a double leg switch while in the air on only one jump.

Lateral Bounds ▶

These exercises are also referred to as "Heidens" after Olympic speed-skating star, Eric Heiden. The motion is similar to one that a speed-skater would make. Bend forward slightly at the waist as you flex the knees. Your arms should be loose at the shoulders but slightly flexed at  the elbow. To execute this drill you should shift your weight fully over to one support leg as you simultaneously cross the swing leg behind the support leg. The arms should come across the body as you cock in preparation for the later bound. As soon as you are stretched and ready, explode laterally across to the other leg and repeat from side-to-side.

Lateral Jumps

These are in the same manner as tuck jumps except you will be moving laterally as well as vertically. You should use normal plyometric technique, except that you will keep your shoulders square and will drive your arms slightly across your body as you jump. Remember to drive the heels and knees-toes up over an imaginary boundary with each repetition.

ChapterSeven

Taking Care of Your Body

Off-Season Conditioning

The best way to make sure that you stay well conditioned is to never get out of shape. It doesn't take very long for someone who is in moderately good condition to get into good enough shape that he can perform in a football practice. As long as you haven't been sitting on the coach eating potato chips for three or four months, it will only take about six weeks to get to a level that will allow you to go to football practice and work your way into top shape from there. If you are a moderately well-conditioned athlete and looking to get in tip-top physical condition, it would probably take eight to twelve weeks.

It's important to compete in other sports when football is out of season. For instance, participation in track and field is a tremendous way to stay in good shape for football. If you are not playing other sports, a two- to three-day-a-week regimen in which you are lifting weights and running is suggested. This will help prepare you for the grind of the football season.

One conditioning drill that can be used in this six-week conditioning program and also as an off-season conditioner is *the gasser*. Start in a three-point stance on one sideline of the football  field. Sprint across the field to the other sideline, touch that line with your foot or your hand, and sprint back to the side you started on. Repeat the process and you have completed one gasser.

Following are off-season guidelines divided by position. Run a minimum of three to four gassers, and as you get in better shape push it to four gassers completed under a specified time (with a one-minute rest in between each one). The guidelines used for NFL players are as follows:

- **Defensive Backs, Wide Receivers and Tailbacks: 37 seconds.**
- **Tight Ends, Linebackers, Fullbacks and Quarterbacks: 39 seconds.**
- **Offensive Linemen and Defensive Linemen: 43 seconds.**

Remember: These times reflect how long it should take to run a complete gasser, which is two trips across the width of a football field and back.

Time yourself in four gassers with a minute rest in between. Write those numbers down and run gassers every day. Time yourself again about a week or so before you report to training camp or football practice. You'll see a big difference.

Injuries

Injuries happen in football. Some happen on the field and some happen in training. Smaller injuries like pulls, strains, and sprains are almost unavoidable, but they do not have to completely disrupt your training. There are a lot of different ways to work out even when you are injured.

An injured athlete can work all of the muscle groups that are not injured. In fact, there's a theory called *bilateral transfer*. It simply means that, for example, if a player has a right arm that has been immobilized—maybe it's in a sling—he can still work on his left arm. Meanwhile, his right arm will still receive about 60 percent of the benefit of working the left side. By working an opposite limb you can help maintain muscle mass in the injured limb.

Whether injuries occur on the field or in the weight room, it's usually because the athlete didn't warm up properly or got sloppy with his technique. Weight room injuries also occur when athletes try to force an exercise or a lift. In other words, they put themselves in a bad position to try to lift too great a weight.

Strain or Sprain?

Strain

The most common weight room injury is the muscle strain. It occurs when a muscle has been extended a little bit further than it can handle and muscle tissue (at a very minor level) has been ruptured. Most strains will be point tender when you push on the muscle. They don't hurt when the muscle is relaxed, but when you try to flex or use the muscle you experience pain.

You'll know right away if you've hurt yourself. The most important thing to do when that happens is to *stop immediately*. This is one of the major reasons why you want to have good, confident spotters because if you need to stop, you can tell them to take the weight. At that time, seek medical attention. If you're at your house or you're at a gym, get some ice and apply it to the sore area. Then visit a doctor and let him or her diagnose the problem. You won't know what happened until someone who has been trained to diagnose those types of injuries can verify that it was a strain, a tear, or just a cramp.

> *You'll know right away if you've hurt yourself. The most important thing to do is to stop immediately.*

The difference between a tear and a strain is quite noticeable. If you have a torn muscle, you will usually notice a hole or an indentation in the muscle. It's very small but it's there, and it causes moderate pain and swelling. A torn muscle means that several of the muscle fibers have given way. They weren't strong enough to hold up, and they've actually torn.

When they do tear, it creates a small hole in the area of the muscle. Tears cause much more severe pain and more swelling then strains. Again, in order to be sure, you need to have to have a qualified health professional take a look and diagnose you. When you feel pain like that, stop immediately, ice it, and seek medical attention.

Sprain

Another common weight room injury—and these often happen on the field as well—are sprains. Whereas tears and strains affect muscle tissue, a sprain involves ligaments and/or tendons. So when we talk about sprains we're usually talking about elbows, shoulders, and ankles. A sprain means that those ligaments and tendons have been stretched beyond capacity and there's some severe irritation involved. Generally, if you have a sprain, there's going to be a sensation of sharp pain. Stop immediately, ice the area, and visit a health professional.

The good news is that most athletes in your age range are able to recover from injuries very quickly. It's important for you to understand what type of injury you have, what your limitations are, and to stay within those limitations as you're trying to rehabilitate.

Don't Over Train

All of these injuries, as well as broken bones, can be the result of over training. That's one of the reasons to always remind yourself that the weight work you are doing is intended to support your efforts on the gridiron. For serious football players, weight lifting is not an end in itself. That's why you should take a total body approach in your training program, precisely so you avoid over training. Over training means that you are working at such a pace over a period of time that your body is not recovering sufficiently enough from one workout to prepare you for the next one.

Some signs of over training are:

- Increased resting heart rate.
- Negative change of body composition. This simply means that over time your body is losing lean muscle. You're putting fat on.

Recovery

Over training can be prevented with a proper recovery. *Recovery* is the amount of time and the quality of time you give to your body after a workout. The most important element in recovery is sleep. Often athletes can't understand why the program they're following is not giving them the results they want. They think it's the plan or the weights or any number of other factors that are holding them back. The answer often turns out to be lack of sleep.

> *Sleep, especially for young athletes, is the most important factor in health and recovery.*

Sleep, especially for young athletes, is the most important factor in health and recovery. You need at least seven to eight hours of uninterrupted sleep every night. Even older athletes sometimes get their schedules so full of daily activities that they forget about the importance of sleep.

Athletes have been taught just to add an extra half-hour of sleep to their nightly schedule, and it has made all the difference in the world. *Note: the key to added sleep is that it has to be made up on the front end during the evening, not the back end during the next morning.* That means going to bed at 10:00 in the evening instead of 10:30, not waking up a half-hour later in the morning.

While sleep is one form of recovery, giving your muscles time before the next workout is necessary too. That's why you shouldn't lift weights every day. The general thinking is to allow forty-eight hours of recovery time between working muscle groups. That can be varied depending upon the intensity and duration of exercise, but at a young age, you definitely want to try to stay within that parameter.

Lifting weights alone does not necessarily make you stronger. It's the rest and nutrition in combination with the weights that make you stronger. As the next section explains, regardless of how old you are, you need to get enough protein to help your body repair itself and become stronger from training. You could do a test with any exercise—say, a squat or a bench press. After working out for two-and-a-half hours and doing 800 reps of squats and 800 reps of bench press you could take a test to see if you were stronger at the end than you were at the beginning. You wouldn't be as strong at the end of that workout as you were at the beginning. But, if you took a couple of days off and provided your body with proper rest and nutrition, when you came back you would undoubtedly be stronger.

Nutrition

As important as sleep and muscle recovery may be, they can't do the job alone. The other key to recovering and fully benefiting from any type of workout is nutrition.

It's very important that you have a good source of protein for breakfast. You can get that from eating eggs or drinking a good protein shake. Protein shakes are low in fat, and have some carbohydrates and protein as well as some fruit. You have to remember the energy you're going to be burning this afternoon is what you took in for your breakfast this morning. If you're running on an empty stomach, don't expect to have a lot of energy in the middle to late afternoon when you're doing your training. A classic balanced breakfast is a great way to start the day. Add to that breakfast a good multi-purpose vitamin and you're all set.

Many of you have grown up eating cereal. There are healthy cereals, but most of the brands young people tend to like are full of sugar. This means that a bowl of those cereals represents a lot of empty calories. They're not adding protein or adding vitamins or minerals. They're just adding empty sugar calories, which doesn't give you much energy to train on.

A Three-Pronged Approach for Good Nutrition:

1. Take a multi-purpose vitamin every day.

The way foods are processed these days, the nutrients that were once in foods are no longer there. In the twenty-first century we don't prepare foods with optimal nutrition in mind; we tend to prepare foods with speed, ease of preparation, and consumption

> *A classic balanced breakfast is a great way to start the day*

in mind. That's why you need to take a multi-purpose vitamin every day. It helps you make up for what the modern-day diet lacks.

2. Eat breakfast every day.

If you don't have the time to get up and cook a breakfast high in protein, then you should take some form of a protein powder or shake that does contain protein. Some people will take a protein powder and actually mix it into pancake batter.

The advantage of a drink is that it's easy to make and is more readily absorbed or digested because it's already in liquid form. How much protein should you ingest on a daily basis? As a guideline, take your weight and multiply that by between .5 and 1. That is approximately the number of grams of protein you should ingest in a day. You can divide that number into several different feedings so your body doesn't have to handle a large amount of protein at any one time.

3. Have a carbohydrate/protein drink after your workout.

Experience has shown—and it has also been fairly well documented—if you can eat a good quality protein-carbohydrate meal fifteen to thirty minutes after training, there seems to be a nutritional window that opens up and allows the body to utilize those components rather quickly. This actually enhances recovery. If you do this on a regular basis, you're going to find that this will reduce muscle soreness, and you'll feel like you are recovering faster.

Some people think they can get away without focusing on their diet. They're wrong. What you're really doing with a bad diet is limiting your potential for strength development and for growth. If you were planting a garden and wanted to have the best garden around, you wouldn't just stick plants in the ground and leave it to chance to see whether they would get watered or whether they would

> **What you're really doing with a bad diet is limiting your potential for strength development and for growth.**

receive vitamins and minerals. You would cultivate them. You would plant them in the right type of soil. You would make sure there was plenty of water available. You would probably put some plant food in the soil. You would water and care for those plants on a regular basis. Your body needs to be cultivated in the same way. You need to oversee your physical development by giving yourself every opportunity to develop—providing yourself with the nutrition that your body needs at the appropriate time. It becomes a cycle. If you're not recovering well, you can't train as hard as you would like to train. When you can't train hard, you won't train as often. When you can't train as often, results are going to be diminished.

Calories

A *calorie* is the smallest unit of measurement when you're talking about nutrition. What is a calorie? When we talk calories, we're actually talking about a unit of heat. In order to create that heat, work or exercise has to be performed. Technically, a calorie is the amount of heat needed to raise one liter of water by one degree centigrade. How do people determine how many calories are in food? They have a device called a calorimeter. You can put a piece of food in that device, saturate it with oxygen, light it, and it burns. It burns everything that's in there. That amount of heat is measured.

Your caloric output can be measured. For every molecule of oxygen that you breathe in, you breathe out one molecule of carbon dioxode. So when studies are done to determine caloric expenditure, they normally put you on a treadmill or stationary bicycle. They hook a tube up to your mouth and they measure how much carbon dioxide your body expends. Then they calculate how many calories that you're burning. A larger individual who has to move more mass is going to burn more calories than a smaller individual, but it basically comes down to the formula of 3,500 calories equals one pound.

The same formula holds if you're trying to add weight. When dealing with college athletes, the old philosophy used to be, "Let's get as much weight on these guys as we can and then we'll trim the fat later." That philosophy seems to have changed over time. Now college athletes are expected to add good lean body weight. The only way that you can do that is to put good fuel in your body. It's like an automobile. You put good fuel in and it burns clean and runs faster. If you put low-quality fuel in, it doesn't burn as clean, and you have a lot more problems.

Now, when you add a lot of fat, you're adding tissue that's not really useful. It's like putting on a weighted vest. To prove this, perform some drills with five or eight pounds of extra weight on and see how you do. Then take that extra weight off. When you're lean, you can perform at a higher level.

Discipline

Of course, the age group you're in has a tendency to eat high fat foods, such as hamburgers and pizza. Also, youngsters eat a lot of sugar. Ultimately, it's all about discipline. It comes down to whether you're going to eat that hamburger or whether you're going to go home and mix up a protein shake. Then you have to stop and reflect: "What am I going to get accomplished by eating this greasy hamburger versus what am I going to accomplish when I go home and take in the proper nutrition? How is that going to affect my recovery from the workout that I just had, and how is it going to affect my ability to prepare for my next workout?" The answers to those questions are clear.

That doesn't mean there's no room in your diet for the occasional treat, but by and large a committed athlete in training has to avoid junk. We've spoken about this before in terms of dedication to weights, but the number one trait that any athlete is going to have to learn is self-imposed delay of gratification. That is, he's got to be willing to work a little harder today because he knows that the reward down the road is going to be greater.

Again, Barry Sanders is an example. Barry's body weight—whether in season or out—never varied by more than three pounds. He had great discipline and a great work ethic, and he developed the trait of self-imposed delay of gratification.

Nutritional Supplements

You may know that a lot of young and veteran athletes alike turn to nutritional supplements to get an edge on their strength training. There are so many supplements on the market that this area can be totally confusing. Furthermore, many of these substances are unsafe and illegal.

However, there are some safe, legitimate brands out there. It's important to steer towards nutritional companies that have partnered with Olympic teams. For instance, look for companies that have partnered with the U.S. Wrestling Team. Olympic athletes have stringent rules that they need to adhere to, and they're not allowed to take illegal or dangerous substances.

If an Olympic team is using and endorsing it, it might be OK, but *check with your physician or a nutritionist before taking any supplement.* The bottom line is that unless you're educated, taking some of these products can be dangerous. Ultimately, you are responsible for what you put in your body.

One interesting development over the last decade or so has been energy bars. These are generally a good source of protein with low fat content. Again, the idea is that they help to supplement your diet. Energy bars do not replace meals, but they can substitute in a pinch. Before you buy an energy bar, read the label. Not all bars are created equal.

Hydration

Finally, the most important fuel for your body is water. The Detroit Lions used to have a rule. They had every player bring a one-gallon jug of water with them to their workout. They kept that jug all day long and tried to drink the entire gallon by the end of the day. When you first start doing it, you have to use the restroom quite often. Your body is not used to trying to hold that additional water, and for most players it took four or five days before they were actually able to finish the entire gallon by day's end. But once you get used to it, it's unbelievable how much more energy you'll have, not to mention how much better you'll feel when you wake up in the morning. Proper hydration also helps you avoid muscle cramping and heat problems, especially during the summer months.

Water is also available in some of the re-hydration drinks now on the market. If you're going to use one of these drinks you should look for one that is balanced one-to-one, potassium-to-sodium. That may be the best combination to help get fluids into your system faster. When you have a combination of sodium and potassium like that, the fluid actually goes through the cells in the stomach and gets in your system faster than water alone.

We tend to drink when we're thirsty, but thirst in itself is a sign that we've waited too long to drink. Basically, it's an early indication that you're at risk. Another more severe symptom of dehydration is muscle cramping. Anyone who has been involved in athletics has probably experienced a cramp. The worst-case scenario is heat stroke, in which your body gets so overheated that it just shuts down. You want to avoid heatstroke at all costs (it can be fatal), so make sure you have plenty of fluids on hand when you work out.

The Dangers of Steroids

An *anabolic steroid* is the familiar name for a man-made substance that exaggerates the effects of natural male hormones. Anabolic steroids were developed in the late 1930s for medical purposes. During the 1930s, scientists discovered that anabolic steroids could also speed the growth of skeletal muscle in laboratory animals. This discovery led to the use of the compounds first by bodybuilders and weightlifters and then by athletes in other sports.

This type of steroid abuse has become widespread in athletics. More than 100 different anabolic steroids have been developed, but they require a prescription to be used legally in the United States. Most steroids that are used illegally are smuggled in from other countries, illegally diverted from U.S. pharmacies, or synthesized in clandestine laboratories. *They are extremely dangerous and should be avoided at all costs.*

One of the main reasons people give for abusing steroids is to improve their performance in sports. Another reason people give for taking steroids is to increase their muscle size and/or reduce their body fat. This group includes some people who have a behavioral syndrome (muscle dysmorphia) in which a person has a distorted image of his or her body. Men with this condition think that they look small and weak, even if they are large and muscular. Similarly, women with the syndrome think that they look fat and flabby, even though they are actually lean and muscular. Finally, some adolescents abuse steroids as part of a pattern of high-risk behaviors. These adolescents also take risks such as drinking and driving, carrying a gun, not wearing a helmet on a motorcycle, and abusing other illicit drugs.

In the United States, supplements such as dehydroepian-drosterone (DHEA) and androstenedione (street name "Andro") can be purchased legally without a prescription through many commercial sources including health food stores. Little is known about the side effects of steroidal supplements, but if large quantities of these compounds substantially increase testosterone levels in the body, they also are likely to produce the same dangerous side effects as anabolic steroids.

Anabolic steroid abuse has been associated with a wide range of adverse side effects ranging from some that are physically unattractive, such as acne and breast development in men, to others that are life threatening, such as heart attacks and liver cancer. Most are reversible if the abuser stops taking the drugs, but some are permanent. In males, these dangerous side effects include infertility, development of breasts, shrinking of the testes, excessive growth of body hair, male-pattern baldness, short stature, tendon rupture, heart attacks, enlargement of the heart's left ventricle, cancer, acne and cysts, HIV/AIDS (from shared needles), oily scalp, homicidal rage, mania, and delusions.

Hormone Disruption

Steroid abuse disrupts the normal production of hormones in the body, causing both reversible and irreversible changes. Changes that can be reversed include reduced sperm production and shrinking of the testicles (testicular atrophy). Irreversible changes include male-pattern baldness and breast development (gynecomastia). In one study of male bodybuilders, more than half had testicular atrophy, and more than half had gynecomastia.

Damaged Musculoskeletal System

Rising levels of testosterone and other sex hormones normally trigger the growth spurt that occurs during puberty and adolescence. Subsequently, when these hormones reach certain levels, they signal the bones to stop growing, locking a person into his or her maximum height. When a child or adolescent takes anabolic steroids, the resulting artificially high sex hormone levels can signal the bones to stop growing sooner than they normally would have done.

Damaged Cardiovascular System

Steroid abuse has been associated with cardiovascular diseases (CVD), including heart attacks and strokes, even in athletes younger than thirty. This happens because steroids can alter the levels of lipoproteins that carry cholesterol in the blood. If blood is prevented from reaching the heart, the result can be a heart attack. If blood is prevented from reaching the brain, the result can be a stroke. Steroids also increase the risk that blood clots will form in blood vessels, potentially disrupting blood flow and damaging the heart muscle so that it does not pump blood effectively.

Liver Disease

Steroid abuse has been associated with liver tumors and a rare condition called peliosis hepatis, in which blood-filled cysts form in the liver. Both the tumors and the cysts sometimes rupture, causing internal bleeding.

Unhealthy Skin

Steroid abuse can cause acne, cysts, and oily hair and skin.

Infection

Many abusers who inject anabolic steroids use nonsterile injection techniques or share contaminated needles with other abusers. In addition, some steroid preparations are manufactured illegally under non-sterile conditions. These factors put abusers at risk for acquiring life-threatening viral infections, such as HIV and hepatitis B and C. Abusers also can develop infective endocarditis, a bacterial illness that causes a potentially fatal inflammation of the inner lining of the heart. Bacterial infections also can cause pain and abcess formation at injection sites.

ChapterEight

Benefits Beyond Football

I f you are serious about becoming the best football player you can be, you need to engage in a conscientious conditioning program. Hopefully this book has inspired you to work hard and be in the best shape possible. But football is not the only reason for being in good condition. In fact, even if you never play in another football game, there are many good reasons to get yourself in good condition and keep yourself there. Below is only part of a list of conditioning benefits compiled by Dr. Michael Olpin, assistant professor of health and human performance at Weber State University in Ogden, Utah. When you decide to start the program, don't forget to document your first day, and your progress, in your journal that begins on p.107.

The Benefits of Conditioning
Cardiovascular Benefits

1. Increases in the diameter of the blood vessels, allowing blood to move through them more easily, decreases the blood pressure during rest, and decreases the chance for blood clots

2. Increases the amount of blood ejected from the heart with each beat, meaning more oxygen and nutrients get into the cells throughout the body

3. Increases blood flow to the muscles, meaning up to 88 percent more blood during higher intensity aerobic activity

4. Increases in strength of contraction of the heart muscle, helping the heart so that it doesn't have to work as hard

5. Decreases resting heart rate, as much as 10 beats per minute (bpm), meaning the heart does not have to work as hard or as often. (Decrease your heart rate by 10 bpm and your heart beats 5,256,000 fewer beats during one year. That adds up to 262,800,000 beats saved over the next 50 years.)

6. Decreases blood pressure, resulting in a decrease in resting systolic, diastolic, and mean blood pressure

7. Increases the number of red blood cells, providing more oxygen-carrying capacity to the cells, since red blood cells deliver the oxygen through the blood from the lungs

8. Increases capillarization, meaning there are more places for nutrients to pass out of the blood into cells. This increases the transport of nutrients and oxygen into the cells from the blood vessels.

9. Increases the blood hemoglobin, transporting oxygen to the muscle, and carbon dioxide (waste matter) to the lungs (to be exhaled). This means much more efficient use of inhaled air to use the oxygen so you can do more work without getting tired.

10. Increases the strength of cardiac tissue resulting in a stronger heart. A stronger heart means it lasts longer and works better.

Better Body Functions and Metabolism

1. Increases the body's ability to utilize fat as an energy source during physical activity. This results in the ability to do work for longer periods of time. You don't "hit the wall" during long periods of activity.

2. Decreases total blood triglyceride. This will further decrease one's chance of heart problems.

3. Decreases percentage of body fat

4. Allows consumption of greater quantities of food while keeping a proper caloric balance

5. Decreases the recovery time from working out. You can begin the next task sooner after working out, and you don't feel sore as long.

6. Increases the number of enzymes involved in aerobic activity. This allows for greater utilization of nutrients and oxygen, leading to higher energy levels at all work levels.

7. Increases activity in the Krebs Cycle. This cycle produces the bulk of the energy the muscles need for endurance.

8. Increases the diffusion of oxygen capacity in the lungs, which means more oxygen is making it to the cells where they can efficiently produce more energy

9. Increases depth of breathing. Not only is this a more relaxing way of breathing, but it also gets more air into the lower parts of the lungs where greater levels of oxygen exchange occur.

10. Increases ability to supply blood flow to the skin for cooling

Musculoskeletal

1. Increases the thickness of cartilage in the joints

2. Increases the strength of connective tissue such as ligaments and tendons. This decreases the risk of many injuries to locations such as the knee, ankle, shoulder, etc.

3. Increases the size of skeletal muscle which allows for greater strength during a contraction (while flexing)

4. Increases overall muscle strength

5. Increases overall muscle endurance

6. Maintains and increases muscle and joint flexibility

7. Enhances muscle tone and physique

8. Improves body posture

9. Builds and maintains lean body mass, increases overall level of muscle strength

10. Helps to alleviate low-back pain

Mental Function

1. Increases endorphin production. These are hormones produced by the brain which cause a person to actually "feel good."

2. Helps to boost creativity

3. Assists in the process of physical relaxation. The body is forced to go through the exhaustion phase after exercise.

4. Decreases overreaction by "stress" hormones. The body will tend to maintain an equilibrium of adrenaline and cortisol, the hormones which give rise to feelings of "fight or flight."

5. Can help relieve the pain of tension headaches, the most common types of headache

Bonus Benefits

1. Improves athletic performance

2. Develops motor skills; improves efficiency of movement (e.g. running, jumping)

3. Improves balance and coordination

4. Improves decision-making abilities

5. Increases productivity levels at work and school

Conditioning Journal

Date	Drill	How I Did

Conditioning Journal

Date	Drill	How I Did

Conditioning Journal

Date	Drill	How I Did

Conditioning Journal

Date	Drill	How I Did

Conditioning Journal

Date	Drill	How I Did

Conditioning Journal

Date	Drill	How I Did

Conditioning Journal

Date	Drill	How I Did

Conditioning Journal

Date	Drill	How I Did

Conditioning Journal

Date	Drill	How I Did

Conditioning Journal

Date	Drill	How I Did

Conditioning Journal

Date	Drill	How I Did

Conditioning Journal

Date	Drill	How I Did

Conditioning Journal

Date	Drill	How I Did

Conditioning Journal

Date	Drill	How I Did

Conditioning Journal

Date	Drill	How I Did

Conditioning Journal

Date	Drill	How I Did

Conditioning Journal

Date	Drill	How I Did

Conditioning Journal

Date	Drill	How I Did

Conditioning Journal

Date	Drill	How I Did

Conditioning Journal

Date	Drill	How I Did

Conditioning Journal

Date	Drill	How I Did

Conditioning Journal

Date	Drill	How I Did

Conditioning Journal

Date	Drill	How I Did

Conditioning Journal

Date	Drill	How I Did

Conditioning Journal

Date	Drill	How I Did

Conditioning Journal

Date	Drill	How I Did

Conditioning Journal

Date	Drill	How I Did

Conditioning Journal

Date	Drill	How I Did

Conditioning Journal

Date	Drill	How I Did

DVD Index

About the Authors

Bert Hill spent eleven seasons overseeing the Detroit Lions' strength and conditioning program. In addition to this role, Hill spent time assisting with the Lions' offensive line.

Hill originally came to the Lions in March 1990 following his second stint at Texas A&M as strength and conditioning coach. While in College Station, the Aggies won three consecutive Southwest Conference titles between 1985-87.

Hill played linebacker at Marion Military Institute Jr. College in Alabama during 1976-77, and one season at Wichita State in 1978. He earned his bachelor's degree in physical education from Auburn University at Montgomery in 1980. In 1982, Hill received his master's degree in physical education with an emphasis in strength physiology, also from Auburn University.

Bert Hill resides with his family in Dallas, Texas.

Steve Watterson is one of the top strength and rehabilitation experts in the NFL, and is currently in his 17th season as the Tennessee Titans' strength and conditioning coach. In 1999, Steve was appointed to the National Research Council for Health (NRCH) scientific advisory council.

In 1992, Watterson was named Professional Strength and Conditioning Coach of the Year. Before joining the Tennessee Oilers (now Titans), Watterson spent two seasons (1984-85) as the assistant trainer for the Philadelphia Eagles. From 1979-80, he served as the head trainer at Tucson (Arizona) High School before accepting a similar post at Amphitheater High School in Tucson during the 1980-84 seasons. Watterson's other activities have included serving as a trainer at the 1982 Olympic Development Camp and at the National Sports Festival in Colorado Springs in 1983.

He received his bachelor's degree from the University of Rhode Island and his master's degree from the University of Arizona. A native of Newport, Rhode Island, Watterson lives with his wife and children in Brentwood, Tennessee.